Journal of a Reluctant Old Codger

By

Simon Monkey

ISBN: 978-1-329-09766-7

JOURNAL OF A RELUCTANT OLD CODGER

CHAPTER ONE: BEGINNINGS & BEFORE BEGINNINGS

My name is Simon Simpell and I am old. I first realised I had unwittingly crossed the Rubicon, that invisible line between middle-aged usefulness and elderly passenger status, when I was still working. It was the day my boss Smartie, aka Richard B. Smart who is also my life-long best friend, was showing a big cheese from headquarters round the office. He pointed at me and said, 'This is Simon. He's part of the furniture.' The realisation that I had suddenly become a random inanimate object barely worth mentioning hit me hard.

DRAWING: Simon as part of a chair/table/wardrobe.

Soon after, I took early retirement from my job at the advertising agency. The commute was killing me and Smartie, with an arm round my hunched shoulders, convinced me I was slowing down and burnt out. Fire blackened derelict warehouses and warts removed with high-tech lasers initially came to mind but the concept applied to people conjured up a bizarre vision of Spontaneous Human Combustion and a pair of smouldering feet left behind on the floor in a blue haze.

DRAWING: Pair of large, smoke-streaked feet on a kitchen floor surrounded by said blue haze.

Sadly for Simon, two months after I'd retired, Peter Stilton, the big cheese he'd shown round the place, decided that my old friend was burnt out too and slipped his P45 into a leaving card. In what seemed like no time at all both of us were trapped in the minefield of opportunity afforded by sheltered accommodation. By the way, everyone's house has a roof and tiles so why is it that only those old people live in are called sheltered accommodation?

We are warden controlled, like prisoners, only no one patrols at night in case it inconveniences burglars or passing drunks from the Cemetery - the pub not the graveyard - who wouldn't have anywhere to piddle if our doorsteps weren't readily available. The warden herself, Betty Boomslanger, is Australian. She visited me yesterday. I answered the door and there she was, all smiling and, as usual, brimming over with goodwill and bonhomie. She said, 'G'day, Simon, love. How are you cobber this fine sunny morning?' Then, before I could answer, she followed up with, 'That's all right then,' before waving goodbye and knocking on the next door along. If you are upright you are alright in Betty's book and she's wise to both moaning and malingering amongst her charges. She has a large, pink, koala-shaped suggestions box in the community hall which often contains unpleasant, anonymous ones regarding her antipodean birthright and what she might do with herself if she was so inclined. Of late, she has threatened to engage the services of the local plod graphologist in order to root out 'the poison pen people' as she calls them before 'suing their fat butts off for every damn dollar they're worth!'

DRAWING: Betty, large and sour-faced, wearing a traditional hat with corks dangling from it on strings knocking on a door with a boomerang accompanied by Plod and a drippy lawyer.

I hope you won't think I'm down on all Aussies 'cause of the previous - that wouldn't do. On the contrary, they're some of the best folk from criminal stock you could ever wish to meet. I hope I haven't given offence or a gatepost to any of you 'downunderers' out there because, for one thing, you won't buy this book. Mind you, it's great winning the Ashes occasionally instead of always harking back to 1981 and Beefy and Bob. Good old Vaughnie, Strauss and Co - you showed 'em good and proper lads. Still; I'm sure all of you inveterate Pom-bashers restraining your marsupials in the outback will realise it's only my little joke…Tee Hee!

The History of Things 1

I met Richard Smart at big school when we were both 11 years old and, yes, he was a clever Dick. Our first meeting, when he trod on my sore foot in the schoolyard, was pretty much a template for the next fifty-odd years

- some of them very odd indeed. Like everyone else, I looked up to him. At six feet tall he towered over the rest of us. But it was his senseless humour and the fact that I didn't know anyone else at the school that led to our lifelong weirdy friendship.

My friend was what they call laid-back - sometimes annoyingly akin to falling over. Being oversized, Smartie never needed to lash out at anyone - even when they deserved it. He had bad moods occasionally which he blamed on me claiming I 'wound him up.' That said, he prided himself on his self-control and being ultra cool. One day, we were down in the school cellar smoking Woodies (legendary Woodbine ciggies) during break. Ironically, we were sat on a bench surrounded by a mountain of smokeless fuel. I was trying to get under his skin as usual, which hardly ever worked, when I must have said something especially irksome. His super-size fist suddenly appeared before me and closed in on my features like a guided missile. I mopped up blood from my cut lip with a grubby handkerchief and threw my butt, the cigarette one, at him, hoping his trousers or skew-whiff tie would catch fire. He'd taken me by surprise and I was wary of another haymaker coming my way but I needn't have worried. He looked devastated and it was obvious he regretted losing it like he had and letting me get to him. In fact, when the incident came up in conversation forty years later he still looked a picture of guilt and shame. I sort of looked up to him in another way after that. I still wind him up though. After all, what are friends for?

DRAWING: Smartie, a giant key in his back, being wound up like a clockwork toy by a malevolent me sporting a hugely swollen lip.

Smartie was far from an unintelligent yob. He was quite gifted academically but found himself deposited in the same South Chadd sinkhole as me for the same reasons - a deep-rooted resentment of authority and a lazy streak the length of his spine when it came to school work. Smartie was lean with a long face and large protruding cartoon ears. His thick, rectangular, black-rimmed glasses and tousled ginger hair completed the impression of an archetypal geek with attitude. Surprisingly, he took a genuine interest in chemistry and the ongoing space race. He set up his own NASA lab' in an old box room at Smart Ass Towers in downtown Oswaldtwistle. Soon, he'd developed an Anglo-Cuban space program consisting of aluminium rockets manufactured from *Castella* cigar tubes and powered by home-made gunpowder. After one particularly impressive flight into Smartie stratosphere he picked up a rocket before it had cooled down and branded the palm of his hand with the legend 'Havana'. Capitals were the subject in class a few days later and when Cuba came up Smartie answered after a quick glance at his open paw. He was strapped enthusiastically by the teacher, Mr Goering, (a cousin of the late Nazi, Hermann) for cheating. Oops, what a give away!

DRAWING: Che Guevara-like Smartie wearing designer shades and a beret saluting one of his rockets as it rises heavenward. The branded word 'Havana' is visible on the palm of his hand.

By the age of ten Smartie had rigged up a connection to the family landline from the telephone wires outside his bedroom window. This meant he could make free calls to anywhere in the universe. Great if you knew anyone living on Mars or, maybe, in Macclesfield but Smartie didn't. Still, free calls to classmates accumulated along with numbers akin to 'Deirdre, your local dominatrix', whose number was prominent in neighbourhood phone boxes (remember them) in those far-off days. He had little understanding of what Deirdre said but told me she knew Mr Goering, our teacher, whose approval of corporal punishment on a one-to-one basis apparently extended beyond his pupils and the classroom. Smartie was also an inventor and claimed to have built the world's first Tone Generator together with Isaac Flint of 5C whose sad demise after consuming a warm light bulb for lunch (and a mad bet) surprised no one who knew him.

DRAWING: Potty schoolboy scoffing light bulb, chips and peas in front of his mates in the school canteen. A horrified teacher is just arriving in the doorway.

CHAPTER TWO: BOOMRIGGERS

More history of things later. Must tell you about life here in Stalag Apfel

Heights where Smartie and I live just a few doors apart. Firstly, we are not popular with the warden. Betty Boomslanger, 'The Boom', is a super control freak. If you're out when the postman calls she lets herself into your house, steals your mail and steams open the ripest-looking letters. What's more, she makes no bones about it. You can always tell if Betty's interfered with any mails – they're soggy and stamped 'Passed' on the bottom. Not even a perfunctory attempt at a cover up. Of course, no one dares to complain – mainly because we're well aware that if she was sacked we might get someone even worse. Another of Betty's little idiosyncrasies is the weekly fire drill. Council rules state one has to be done every three months but The Boom is hot on fire prevention and insists on one every week, come rain or shine. Last winter, eight of us were hospitalised due to exposure after standing without coats or woolies in Apfel Square during her February drill.

DRAWING: Shivering, scantily-dressed old folk being addressed in the Square by Betty Boomslanger wearing a fur coat, thick gloves and a woolly hat. There is a ticket hanging down from the sleeve of her coat marked RETURN TO OWNER IF FOUND and a picture of a cuddly mink underneath/alongside.

Smartie and I are in love. Not with each other I hasten to add but, rather, our neighbour and fellow inmate of Stalag Apfel Heights, Clovella Skinley. She may be73 but Clovella is a goddess and fiendishly beautiful. Tall and elegant, she has flowing grey hair, ocean-blue eyes, exquisite bone structure and full red lips that form the most perfect pout. I also admit to having an abiding affection for a cute round blemish-mark high on her left cheek half the size of a blueberry - echoes of the gorgeous Lisa Stansfield, a diva I've long had a soft spot for (groan). Clovella is a published author too. Her romantic novella, *Love and Urticaria Under a Finnic Moon,* was a bestseller in Bulgaria where they appreciate a good book. Shamefully, it remains a hidden gem hereabouts. My own copy, a first edition in Bulgarian of course, has pride of place on my bookshelf.

DRAWING: A glamorous Clovella signing copies of her book on a tatty sofa at Sofia airport surrounded by swooning, elderly Bulgars.

Stalag Apfel Heights has a number of strict 'No' policies including pets; smoking; skateboarding; skinny-dipping in the lake; consuming your favourite tipple in public; grassing on The Boom to visitors and the council or contacting her during *Neighbours*. Callers after 9pm are subject to a blistering volley of Aussie abuse, told to sink a stiff drink of elderflower presse and get an early night. If that means a night on the kitchen floor after a fall and you can't get back on your feet - 'tough tittie' as they say in these parts. That said, there isn't an official 'No fraternising' policy that I know of and both Smartie and I would like to fraternise big time with Clovella. I have bought her flowers, red roses no less, while Smartie has tried his luck with an old friend of his from way back when.

Smartie particularly despised geography at the South Chadd sinkhole and was always out to cause trouble in class. The worst trouble he ever caused was with 'Sniffer' his pet 'dog'. Half way through the lesson everyone's attention turned on Smartie's antics. Guffaws and giggles constantly interrupted the wise words of our teach', Mr Rigby. He stopped in mid-sentence and zeroed in on the culprit who carried on regardless. An infuriated Riggers took aim with the piece of chalk in his hand. It flew through the air and lodged painfully in Smartie's ear. He howled, frantically shaking his head from side to side. Riggers wanted to know what he'd been doing but Smartie cocked a deaf 'un. An incandescent Riggers, on his top note, repeated the question. Still shaking his head, Smartie explained…'I'm a bit Mutt and Jeff, sir. Some absolute moron threw a piece of chalk at me and plugged my ear-hole. I was only exercising my dog.' Riggers was taken aback, disbelief and fury chasing each other across his podgy features.

'You have actually brought a dog into class with you, Smart?' My friend grinned.

' I had to, sir. He's attached to me and parting would have been painful.' A bemused Riggers navigated a path to Smartie's desk and looked everywhere. Only books and pens met his gaze. By then, the whole class were in stitches and laughter echoed along the narrow corridor as far as Little Harry in the chemistry lab' and Big Harry of that ilk teaching biology. Riggers demanded to know where Sniffer was and Smartie coolly balanced the two long fingers of his right hand either side of his longer middle finger which twitched from side to side sniffing round and about. The 'dog' walked over to Peter Turner's pencil box whereupon Smartie lifted a finger on one side and vocalised the inevitable outcome of dog meeting lamp post which brought the house down as it were. Soon after, exercising a teacher's inalienable right in those days to administer pretty much any known form of physical punishment, Riggers brought a wooden blackboard duster he was carrying crashing down on Smartie's right hand and the unfortunate Sniffer. It would be a long time before that hapless hound made another appearance in Riggers' geography class.

DRAWING: A horrified Smartie gazing down at the huge red and throbbing fingers of his right hand after the sad demise of Sniffer.

CHAPTER THREE: SCARECROW & THE GREAT BUNK-OFF

Clovella wasn't impressed with Smartie's incontinent pet. Nor my flowers for that matter which had wilted ferociously in no time as I'd forgotten to put them in water overnight. Sadly, it's so much harder to attract the ladies when you're old. Paunches, even small ones, are a big turn-off while thinning hair and bald patches are not far behind. Bitten nails, excess nasal hair or a whiff of halitosis and they're off - sticks and walking frames disappearing in the distance before you can reach for the Listerine. Glam' grannies are hard to please I can tell you and with more men nowadays doing a Bee Gees and staying alive longer they've plenty of us to choose from. Beauty contests for baldies - only a matter of time.

DRAWING: Old, bald guys lined up like girls in an old-fashioned beauty contest holding cards with their numbers in front of them. Some have a leg daintily raised behind them in the air and 'come hither' smiles.

Yesterday afternoon, Smartie and I were joined on a bench in the lakeside garden by Harry Butt (don't bother, he's heard them all before). Harry is a great guy with an eye for the ladies but seriously unlucky. Last Christmas he stepped sideways towards the kerb to avoid walking under a ladder and fell into the road. He was hit by a white van loaded with cages full of rabbits on their way to a local show. If he'd walked under the ladder he wouldn't have been injured and, ironically, rabbits' feet are supposed to bring you good luck.   Those attached to the rabbits in the van didn't bring old Harry any. He crawled back onto the pavement and the next thing along was a ten mph street cleaning machine which would probably have polished his shoes and not much else. Murphy and that law of his have a lot to answer for, methinks.

Even more unluckily, Harry lives directly across from the warden and can't make a move without Betty Boomslanger's beady eye on him. He calls on me most afternoons for a quick fag or three unobserved but, recently, things have taken an ominous turn for the worse and it's clear The Boom is out to nail him. The three of us were about to go for a stroll round the lake when Smartie spotted a movement in some bushes opposite our bench. At first we thought it was Fang, the Heights' black tomcat, out birding or on the razzle again but then we caught a momentary glimpse of a big wide-brimmed hat with corks dangling from it. Clearly, The Boom was on the prowl and Harry would have to forgoe his daily drag which annoyed him no end. Just how much became evident when we finally got up to leave. He turned his back on the bushes, pulled his chinos and boxers down and ruthlessly mooned the enemy. If Betty was shocked she had to take it lying down as it were or, more likely, crouching uncomfortably. Behind her a fish leapt out of the water with a wide grin on its face.

'Did you see that,' I said. 'I think it was a carp or a bream?'

'I don't know,' mused Smartie. 'But I guess it was a bottom feeder.'

The next day Smartie and I met Harry again at the bench to see what would happen. Sure enough, Betty's danglers were visible in the shrubbery and a pair of bird watcher's binoculars glinted at us in the afternoon sunshine.

Harry was for going over and telling her where to get off but Smartie had a better idea and borrowed my mobile. He put in a call to the local plod house and young PC Bray appeared on the scene post haste. We explained that Harry had a stalker observing his every move on a daily basis and she was currently secreted in the bushes nearby. The Boom found herself unceremoniously hooked out of her hidey-hole and her particulars taken down prior to removal to the local nick. She got off with a police caution having friends in high places - the posh upmarket Hillside area of town. A tame councillor, Marion Nett, pulled a few strings with the Chief

Constable on Betty's behalf. (I hope that one didn't pass you by).

DRAWING: Old Harry Butt mooning at Betty in the bushes by the lake. A fish is leaping out of the water grinning manically.

While The Boom was away we came out to play. If only for a few precious hours, Stalag Apfel Heights was truly liberated. Harry Butt, living up to his name, went through a whole pack of ciggies for the Hell of it and I got to play loud music - my grandson's electro-beat *Clean Bandit* album. A gang of us played boules, bad backs notwithstanding, on the carefully manicured communal lawn which was unheard of in Betty's reign. Consequently, no one saw Smartie slink off surreptitiously round the back of the warden's house. Opening the low wooden gate which was on the latch he slipped into the garden where a long line of Betty's washing had been hung out to dry. Smartie opened the bin bag he'd brought along and filled it with Betty's clothes, including some rather daring black stockings and skimpy knickers, before carefully retracing his steps.

Barrow Brook farm is a cockstride away down the lane from Stalag Apfel Heights and the nearest field has a crop of corn growing in it overseen by a 'Worzel' scarecrow whose outfit is mostly pre-war - the Crimean - and a disgrace to any self-respecting frightener of corvidae. Smartie soon smartened him up with The Boom's togs and turned him into a pedigree cross-dresser. Cars and ramblers passing by stopped in their tracks and pictures appeared in the local paper much to the farmer's and Betty's displeasure. The headline was, 'Do You Recognise These Clothes?' Of course, Betty did. But she was too embarrassed to claim them and never looked that scarecrow in the eye (or the groin) again. Everyone at the Heights wondered, sometimes out loud, who the racy underwear might have been purchased to impress? (Another thought passed through Smartie's mind, as it did mine, concerning the curvaceous Clovella. What would she have looked like in the black stockings and skimpy knickers? Be still, my dickey heart.) Betty's shocking stockings and other 'down under' items had surprised the Heights community to the extent that wide-eyed sniggering was rife. And the cherry on the cake was that Betty knew it.

DRAWING: Worzel scarecrow dressed in Betty's togs looking fed up in his field. Shocked young rabbits are staring up at the bizarre sight while their mothers are trying to cover the youngsters' eyes with their paws.

I happened to mention to Smartie how, strangely, I'd almost felt sorry for The Boom seeing her slinking out of the police car and making a run for her house. Then there was the empty washing line and the pics in the paper that followed. Even Harry Butt had said something similar and I asked Smartie if he felt just a smidgeon of guilt about the whole thing. 'Don't be soft,' he said. 'This is war!'

The History of Things 3

Talking about South Chadd, our old sinkhole school, (which, admittedly, I wasn't) it was so bad in those days that the school badge featured a cat o' nine tails and a stout cane with the legend *lasciate ogni speranza, voi che'ntrate* - abandon all hope ye who enter (Dante's *Inferno:* from the inscription over the gate of Hell). Fortunately, most of us served our time there without ever knowing its meaning though we experienced its implications on a daily basis.

It was pretty cool at our school to 'bunk off' now and then and miss a day's lessons. Taking the unauthorised time out was laughably easy. The next day you handed your teach' a 'parental' note in the best handwriting of Spud Williamson of 5A who was happy to oblige in exchange for a Hollands' meat pie from the chippy or a *Mambo* or *Jubbly* from the corner shop. These were a real money-maker for Jock McFadden who owned the place consisting, as they did, of large blocks of ice coloured with orange juice diluted to almost homeopathic levels. Jock liked to live up to everyone's image of the archetypal Scotsman and it was no secret that he collected the small round pink and blue hundreds and thousands that fall off certain types of liquorice allsort, bagged them up and sold them on. Spud's notes usually passed muster and Smartie had one that was top drawer. His bright idea was to go to Victoria station and catch the first local train to wherever the first local train was going which would have been fine except the first local train was going to Wacup. Wacup (pronounced way cup) is the sort of place snow likes to fall. It gets cut off in summer, never mind winter, and this was January. It's backward and bleak - a sort of English Fargo nowheresville. People who live there say they live in Warrendale to avoid actually mentioning Wacup. Still; in those days, even Wacup seemed preferable to history via 'Snotty' Platt with his leaky nose and dead-pan delivery. As we sat contentedly in our seats staring out of grimy windows eating fruit pastilles large flakes of snow began to fall outside and the sky turned deeply grey.

'Don't like the look of that,' said Smartie. 'The sky's the colour of your underpants!'

'At least my mum doesn't have to soak the skid marks out of mine before they go in the wash.' Cue chaotic satchel fight in carriage only interrupted by the train pulling out of the station at the speed of slime exiting from a geriatric, arthritic slug.

DRAWING: A 'slug train' containing two satchel-wielding combatants chugging out of the station wearily.

We were probably half way to Wacup looking out on a white landscape when the train slowly ground to a halt. No station was in sight and there was no announcement as to what the problem might be. An hour and innumerable games of 'Hangman' later, the train still hadn't moved. We took a walk up and down and discovered that we were the only passengers aboard.

''Nobody about,' I burbled.

'We're on a g-g-ghost train!' stammered Smartie.

'Rubbish!'

'Just wait. A headless figure carrying an axe will suddenly appear.

Headless blokes with axes always come through the wall.'

'There aren't any walls,' I pointed out.

'Oh! We'll probably be all right then.'

We entertained ourselves with a few games of I-Spy on our return to the

carriage. Looking outside, all I could spy began with an *s* which I stupidly

used and Smartie guessed immediately. He spied a *g* and I had to admit

defeat five baffling minutes and several half-hearted attempts later. Smug

and self-satisfied, he stretched his long spindly legs and gazed out of the

window at a view that by then had pretty much turned into a picture on the

wall.

'Well?' I demanded.

'Well…what?'

'What's the answer?' He looked at me in that odd way he had that

suggested both puzzlement and a certain snobby superiority that always

got right up my schnozzle.

'To the universe? Life on Earth?' he mused. 'Or why Linda Lewis never

lets you fondle her baps like she lets me?'

'Bastard!' I bellowed, angry because it was true. I resolved there and then

that the next time I saw her I'd sneak up on the lovely Linda, grab a hold

of those bosom beauties and hang on for dear life till she shook me off.

After all; it was only fair - her always letting Smartie cop a handful in Art class when Miss Barnes had her back to us at the blackboard. I quickly changed the subject.

'What did you spy?' I asked him.

'Oh, that…a ghost. Didn't you clock him…the headless bloke outside the window?'

'No.'

'He couldn't get in as it wasn't a wall. He looked pretty cheesed about that and started twiddling the axe in his right hand. You must have seen him.' I gave up and, out of habit, looked down at my busted Timex watch. I shook it till my arm ached but the hands never budged. As far as my watch was concerned it would always be 10.37 on Tuesday. It must have given up the ghost (as Smartie should have done) during mouldy Miss Hampson's biology class - probably bored into submission by her vain attempts to impart knowledge in a droning monotone to an almost comatose flock. No sex classes either in those days to keep us awake. Mind you, Hammy on birds, bees and bonking would have been a tad incongruous - akin to Nero on fire-fighting for dummies.

DRAWING: An aged, drab-dressed, scowling female teacher pointing to a blackboard illustration of Adam and Eve who are looking perplexed. A manic, sweating Nero is fiddling furiously behind them with flames licking at his toga.

'What time is it?' said Smartie.

'Same as always…10.37 on Tuesday'. We burst out laughing and the snow continued to fall outside filling in the few gaps of bare landscape it had left before. There were still no signs of train life, like us moving or a guard or a ticket collector coming along.

'I've had it with sitting here,' announced Smartie. 'I'm pulling that cord over there.'

'You dumb cluck,' I yelled. 'Are you a complete idiot or is there a bit missing?'

'It's a communication cord, isn't it? he pointed out. 'Well, I want to communicate with someone - anyone, really.' I told him to leave it alone but, needless to say, he went ahead and pulled it.

Smartie got his wish but he might have been more careful what he wished for. There was a heavy tramp of footsteps in the corridor and an angry, big-bellied guard looked into our carriage. He seemed surprised, if not pleased, to see us.

'Now…what's this then?' he began. 'Was it you as pulled that cord?' Smartie, clocking the irate guard as a local oik and turnip-trampler, put on a posh voice and manners.

'Listen, my man. What's going on with this choo-choo? We should have been in blessed Wacup by now.'

'Niver you mind Wacup, young 'un. Did you pull that there cord or did you not? That's strickly fer emergency as you should know'. Clearly, Smartie's Buck House banter hadn't placated the railway plod who looked distinctly unimpressed.

'This is an emergency,' insisted Smartie.' We haven't eaten since brekker and we're starving'.

'Well, you can eat your words then, young 'un. You two are coming with me'. The guard's chubby fingers closing on my left ear is a painful reminder of that trip. The memory has stayed with me into old age and,now and again, still gives me the sweats at night.

Smartie and I were taken to a nearby village where we were unceremoniously dumped in a leaky shelter to wait for a bus back to the city - still starving and freezing cold to boot. The guard had made a note of our details including our school and told us he'd be ringing the headmaster which was okay really as we told him we went to Royton & Crompton and our names were Harley and Davidson. On the bus I called Smartie every bad name I could think of, which were many and included dumb gizzard, and refused his offer of a half-sucked gobstopper. He claimed what had happened was an 'act of God' and denied all responsibility which was pure Smartie really. I reminded him that the guard had threatened him with prosecution and he'd nearly been the first person charged with pulling a communication cord to stop an already stationary train. The silver lining, of course, would have been a day off school to attend court.

DRAWING: A judge wearing a black cap saying, "Richard Smart…you will be taken to the nearest passenger train and secured by the communication cord, all sustenance denied, until your trousers fall down and we can all have a giggle".

CHAPTER FOUR: BANANAS AND BEAKERS

Smartie and I have come full circle. When we were kiddoes I was the sporty one, always playing or watching footie, cricket, rugger or tennis. I even watched the annual Oxford and Cambridge boat race on the Beeb, possibly the most mind-bogglingly boring non-event ever devised by man, while Smartie was strictly anti-sport - in fact anti-anything sweaty or remotely competitive. Now; he's an obsessive walker, cyclist and all round pain in the ass fitness freak and I - well, I just write, usually with a cold beer or a glass of Chilean merlot in the immediate vicinity. The only exercise I get is going over and turning the TV on: because I've lost the remote again. It always turns up eventually and I always lose it again. This is not related to old age or memory loss - just casual stupidity.

Smartie and I follow our local non-league footie team - Watling Street Bananas. We're seasoned ticket holders having been in the stand, where oddly you sit, forever it seems. The team was founded by some dockers before they were all made redundant by the Blessed Margaret in her heyday. The lads were much impressed by clubs with bonkers names like Plymouth Argyle, Sheffield Wednesday, Leyton Orient and, of course, the daddy of all exotically named clubs, Accrington Stanley. As the docks were off Watling Street and they'd unloaded crates of the fruit that morning they naturally put two and two together and The Bananas were founded. Since then, they have risen up the footie pyramid as far as the

Very Small Places League North, Division Nine. Last year they drew the mighty Centurions of Cirencester Town in the Almost But Not Quite Preliminary Round 0.5 of the FA Cup. For The Bananas it was like drawing Arsenal or Liverpool at home and their joy was unconfined. A sponsor, hitherto unknown, appeared on the scene in the form of a bloke brewing beer in his garden shed. He paid for the team's new strip. Gone was the traditional large yellow fruit on the sacred black shirts replaced by a frothing pint glass of beer and 'Cadwaller's *Oily Clog!* Brewed For Real Men' below. They've started selling *Oily Clog* in the local supermarket but I've never bought a bottle. It's the skull and crossbones on the label that puts you right off - not to mention the pic' of a coffin being lowered into a grave and 22 per cent alcohol inscribed underneath. The Bananas have really lived up to their name with that one,

I reckon.

We got thrashed 16-0 by The Centurions who demonstrated an inexplicable lack of sportsmanship at the end of the game. For some reason they refused to exchange shirts with The Bananas and left the pitch to the jeers of the home fans - all thirty-one of us. (Actually, only thirty of us jeered as Walter Swinbourne's recent throat op' had reduced him, temporarily at least, to a painful squeak). Their single - in the sense of their only being one - supporter, a bloke called Terry, clapped, cheered and generally exhibited euphoria at The Centurions great victory. We left him celebrating in an empty stadium and hurried home to watch Doctor Who on television.

DRAWING: Diamond geezer Terry exhibiting said euphoria in a school playing field of a 'stadium' with banana-shaped goalposts.

The History of Things 4

I've been thinking. Maybe I have been too hard on the South Chadd sinkhole. Maybe it was just me. After all, Smartie, Pete Berry, Jennifer Mills and brain box Marilyn Blake got a few O-levels out of it. I took five of them and failed the lot. I was absolutely, abysmally naff. Before the exams I'd been awarded a *Certificate for the Most Improved Pupil*. How bad must I have been to get that?

Strange to relate, I was in the top A class throughout my time in the sinkhole though, in year 3, I suddenly found myself demoted to B stream. Devastating but fully deserved, I admit. I took my designated place amongst the B worthies with a face as glum as a glow-worm under a sun lamp. I wouldn't say they were thickoes - not in those days anyway - as most of them were bigger than me and would have beaten me black and blue. But they were complete strangers and generally regarded as one step up the evolutionary ladder from pond life. They looked none too pleased that September morning to see an erstwhile A streamer in their midst and I got the distinct impression that they couldn't wait for lunch break to make my life a misery. Then; it happened. Little Harry, a mainly A stream teach', appeared in the doorway and told me to rejoin my mates in my old classroom. Unexpectedly, the decision to demote me had been reversed. I never knew why but I was made up about it. I left the gobsmacked B streamers, sorely robbed of their prey, with my nose in the air and a triumphant kiss-my-ass gesture behind my back that even they understood. It felt good to be back with my old A stream buddies but, strangely, they seemed less than ecstatic at my return to the fold. Even Smartie only gave me a quick nod and something of a sickly smile. Weird. One day I'll get round to asking him what was behind the lukewarm reception but, to date, I've always been a tad afraid of the answer.

Little Harry was a brilliant teach' who actually cared about the kids in his class - almost unheard of in the South Chadd sinkhole. Though not diminutive, he was the smaller of the two Grundys teaching at our school, the other being Big Bald Bill - maths and woodwork. Harry got you motivated by making lessons interesting and cool but, above all, through the trust he invested in you. When he handed out homework he issued no threats, dire or otherwise. It was all about not letting him down. And we rarely did. A gang of us spent our break times with him in the science lab' sipping coffee from glass beakers and talking shop and football. It was football that Harry came over to discuss with me one day. He was in charge of the school first team and I was the star left winger. I thought teamwork and tactics would be on the agenda but he looked serious and preoccupied.

'Simon…I've been thinking. I'd like to give Freddie Sweeney a chance on the wing against Breezehill this week. He's been sharp in training lately.'

'I see.' (Translation: 'Come on, Harry…Freddie Sweeney? Might as well play Sweeney Todd. Freddie's a goon with one gonad - hopeless with the ball at his feet.')

'It'll probably be for the one game.'

'I understand.' (Translation: 'Do I Hell! One game, my cushion-crusher. Losing my place sucks but losing it to frog-faced Freddie - no way!')

'I must say, Simon, you're taking this very well. Credit to you.'

'It's your decision. I totally respect that.' (Translation: 'I'm a skinch off blubbing like a baby. I bet Bobby Charlton never got left out by his teach. You've ruined my life, Harry.')

As it turned out, Freddie flopped. Having fallen over in the penalty area, the ball was crossed in front of him. He stuck out his foot and, literally, missed a sitter as the ball headed for the corner flag. Later, he contrived to balloon an attempted clearance over our keeper's head and notched up a spectacular own goal for good measure. I was reinstated for the next fixture against our old enemy, the North Chadd kickers. Kickers wasn't part of their name but what they did. Our narrow 2-1 victory came at a cost. Six of us ended up in A&E and I bruised a rib which was more painful than actually breaking one. To be precise, their hefty right back bruised it for me but I couldn't have cared less. I was back in the team and all was well with the world. On the plus side, temporarily at least, I'd gained Harry's respect and demonstrated fortitude under the pressure of his flawed, not to say fatuous, team selection. On the other hand, breathing was a problem. Still; I did enough of it to survive and write these memoirs so fair do's.

DRAWING: Hospital ward full of young footballers with multitudinous injuries sticking pins in North Chadd dolls.

If one incident summed up Little Harry it was the Great Gambling Ban. The Head teach', Hoppy Hilton (one leg blown off by a fart mine in the war - probably of The Roses), had heard the all-too-true tales of gambling with cards FOR MONEY that some of his more enterprising pupils were engaged in during lunch breaks. Sucking up to the governors, in this case a couple of dodgy councillors he went to the races with at Haydock Park, he decided to clamp down on nefarious activities of the sort in the sinkhole. Harry warned us about breaking Hoppy's ban on gambling and put us on trust to kick it in touch. He knew, of course, that we were among the culprits but, personally, saw no great harm in it given the small sums involved.

Evan Welch organised our penny pontoon circle. A lethal combination of obstinacy and stupidity made him determined that it should not only survive but thrive 'underground' as he put it. This turned out to be the coke cellar - haunt of inglorious smoke heads a la Smartie and me. The irony was that Evan was a lousy pontooner and usually lost when he played. It's fair to say that most of us took pennies from Evan on a regular basis (groan).

It will come as no surprise that Harry, puzzling on the almost genocidal disappearance of his class one lunch-time, decided to investigate and quickly discovered our subterranean hidey-hole. The look on his face as he stepped down into the cellar was melancholic rather than furious.

'I suppose you know what I'll have to do now,' he mumbled. 'Follow me.'

Back in the classroom, racked with shame and guilt at having let him down, we queued in an orderly line to be strapped, our sweaty hands clenching and unclenching in anticipation.

'This is going to hurt me more than you,' he announced. No one doubted it in the least. It should have been six stingers across the palms of the hands but Harry left it at two each. When it was over he departed for the staff room, head bowed in silence. I don't recall any of us abusing his trust ever again.

CHAPTER FIVE: SHOUT!

One thing, among many, that annoys me about getting old is no go areas. Not the ones in run down city centres or the stairwells of dingy tower blocks, I mean the ones on your body. It's harder to reach and clean all the creases and crevices when you're old. You have to be careful round the crown jewels of course and avoid damaging the moles and skin tags under your armpits that seem to proliferate over the years. Interestingly (or not), some spies are called moles but there are none called skin tags that I know of. Be that as it may, dexterity is at a premium with the advancing years and your favourite, skilfully-wielded loofah comes in very handy I can tell you.

DRAWING: Oldster with a large loofah doing a 'Twister' to reach improbably difficult bodily locations.

One day I was sitting admiring the Google map pattern of liver spots on my left arm when Smartie arrived for our usual afternoon stroll. These strolls sometimes turned into long meandering walks and, occasionally, convoluted bus rides. That day our route took us through the garden and down by the lake where we spotted The Boom haranguing Lily Macduff for burying her granddaughter's hamster in the back garden. Apparently, the aforementioned 'no' list at Staleg Apfel Heights extended to the burial of a relative's small mammal on your own patch of council turf. Typically, the Aussie harridan was taking no prisoners, even mild-mannered octogenarian ones, when it came to dubious rule breaking.

'Now, Lily, me old pommie princess. You know the rules.'

'Not all of them. The rule book's thicker than *Fifty Shades of Grey'* said Lily, sticking up for herself.

'That's as maybe…What did you say?' began Betty. 'Have you been reading that lurid trash, Lily?'

'Well, the library didn't have *Tropic of Cancer* so I asked for that one. But they hadn't got that either.'

'That book is obscene.'

'Oh, you've read it then?' trilled Lily, unfazed and unperturbed.

'I - I - I read the review in the *Daily Femail*. Absolutely disgusting, I believe.'

'Whatever you say, Betty. Let's just bury the hatchet along with the wee hamster, shall we?'

'Bonzer!' yapped The Boom. Turning quickly, she was off on her rounds. But before she was out of hearing Lily shouted at the top of her voice…'My name's down at the library for *Fifty Shades of Grey* when you take it back!'

That Lily - SuperMacs 1, Downunderers 0.

We took a rest on Harry Butt's bench and absent-mindedly discussed memorials. The Butt bench itself was in fact a memorial to a former Heights rezi' by the name of Clarence Clink. Neither of us believed that was his real name but it turns out it was. A small brass plaque screwed to the back rail announced that Clarence had been 'a very special man'. Rumour had it that Clarence and Betty had been an item before his heart attack and The Boom had paid for the plaque herself. Seems like Betty and clink were just fated to be bedfellows. Suddenly, it felt chillingly cold on that bench and we resumed our walk. We hadn't gone far when we heard old Dawkin Luxton's voice though the man himself wasn't visible. Dawkin, of Devonish origin, had found solace and civilisation up North after a lifetime of backbreaking agricultural toil. He didn't suffer fools or his bad back gladly.

'What's that, woman? I can't hear you.' he yelled. There was no reply. 'Speak up!' he bellowed. Still nothing. Smartie and I thought old Dawkin had taken to talking to himself but then we heard a faint whisper. It was Betty Boomslanger's voice but she was decidedly not booming on this occasion. We manoeuvred into a position where we could see as well as hear them. Every time Dawkin said anything Betty answered in a whisper until, finally, he was convinced he was going deaf. During the next few weeks we kept meeting folk who were wearing newly bought hearing aids

-all of a naff design even the NHS would have been ashamed to supply.
All of them believed their hearing was failing after meeting up with Betty.
They had all bought 'bargain' hearing aids off her that were made by a
company that, appropriately, no one had heard of. Looking at the receipts,
they were expensive bargains. Clearly, Betty had been getting a
substantial Boomslanger backhander from the firm, Dezibel, to supply
their puny products to as many of her charges as she could. Betty was one
dodgy Sheila gone bad. Then again, maybe it was Aussie revenge -
sending us their criminals to see how we like it. Fair dinkum, I suppose,
but Smartie and I didn't like it. We didn't like it at all.

DRAWING: Lots of oldsters wandering around the Heights
garden/lake area sporting huge, ugly-looking hearing aids making their
heads lean to one side with the weight of them.

A week of worry later, Smartie was about to tear his hair out and admit
defeat. He just couldn't concoct a decent plan to spike The Boom and
Dezibel that would serve them right, left and sideways for ripping off our
neighbours and friends. As usual, I wasn't much help but I did have a
secret weapon - my grandson Jack - who was a gadget geek and knew his
way round computers like the smartest Applemonger or Microsoft Man.
Jack's a good lad but could be persuaded to do something dodgy in a good
cause by his rascally old grandad. While he was hacking into The Boom's
computer Smartie and I had a word with Trading Standards. We went on
to organise a mass demo' outside Dezibel's headquarters in the town

centre. It took off big time. In our neighbourhood, there wasn't a sheltered house sheltering anybody on the appointed day and a large contingent turned up from various oldie organisations we'd written to for support. Unexpectedly, hordes of students from the nearby uni' joined in and turned up the volume of protest enough to stop traffic and attract camera crews from the Beeb and elsewhere. Placards magically appeared...'Deafinitely Dodgy' and 'Dezibel Hell' among them. The firm's chief executive, Jack Slicer, was a well-known local businessman hence the 'Jack the Rip off!' slogans. That evening there was a well attended concert to raise funds for victims of Dezibel featuring half a dozen Manchester bands playing under the banner of 'Hearing Aid'. Oldsters could hand in their hyper-expensive hardware and get handsomely compensated from the money raised plus free copies of the bands' latest CDs namely Dirty Washing's *Nuclear Detergent'*; Incontinent Panda's *'Bamboo Leaf Bog Roll'*; The Dire Beetees *'Millie Molls with Machine Guns Killed The Krays'* and Tiny Members' *'Surgical Enhancement'*. The Police (group not plods) threatened to reform and sent a message - in a bottle floating down the Ship Canal - that never arrived. We even tried to get a question asked in parliament at PMQs but never found an 'honourable' member to ask it. Meanwhile, grandson Jack had hacked into Betty's inflated bank account and transferred all her ill-gotten gains to the Deaf Society as a philanthropic donation. It didn't take long for The Boom to discover she'd gone bust but with fraud squaddies investigating the whole scam she sagely decided to keep shtum and clear of clink by virtue of an empty bank account.

The History of Things 5

Our dog days in the South Chadd sinkhole coincided with the early

Sixties and the birth of The Beatles. Everyone had their favourite Beatle

(inexplicably, mine was Ringo) and the release of a new single by the band

was a world event. Their impact in the realms of music and fashion was a

global earthquake way off the Richter scale. Believe me, not the pseudo

statistics you might have read, it has never been repeated and, probably,

never will be. One day, Smartie and I walked home with Billy Lloyd who

had asthma and brains. He was almost certainly smarter than Smartie but

less of an asshole and quiet with it. His mum had one of those old record

player cabinets which looked like a simple piece of grotesque furniture.

You opened its front doors to access the player itself. Mrs Lloyd had just

bought the new Beatles single *From Me To You* and Billy invited us

indoors to hear it. Incredible. There was no homework done that night (the

norm anyway for me). We were all coppering up our loose change to

purchase our own six shillings and sixpence copies of The Beatles record

the next day.

The Beatles, more than anyone else, were responsible for inflicting aural

carnage upon our proverbial green and pleasant. Not by their own efforts,

of course, but those of others trying, haplessly and hopelessly, to emulate

them. The Fabs could play but the fatuous and the fantasists couldn't.

Every kid from eleven to nineteen and older was out to form or join a band

and all too many of us did - including me and Smartie. The electric guitar was the favoured instrument of torture and copies of Bert Weedon's *Play in a Day* sold like all-day breakfasts in a famine. No one I knew actually played guitar in a day but mastering three chords in a fortnight qualified you as the neighbourhood Eric Clapton and the cream of a rag, tag and bobtail crop of wannabe musos. Smartie, naturally, mastered the guitar in a couple of months while I was a teenage prodigy when it came to the tambourine and writing dumb lyrics for the attempted songs we put together. Unwisely, some recordings were made on my reel-to-reel tape recorder at the time which, if they fell into record company hands, I still like to think could lead to senior citizen stardom (in deluded moments).

DRAWING: Two oldsters with white beards down to the ground age-jiving with their instruments on stage in front of a comatose audience.

We called ourselves DNA B - band spelt backwards - which was frequently interpreted as Do Not Approach   Bastards! Scouring the area for gigs whilst hardly ever rehearsing, we stumbled across The Wheatsheaf in Manchester. It was basically a folk venue where we were hardly likely to go down well with the steely-eyed spanners who made up most of the audience but hope springs a leak in the urinal and DNA B were booked for a spot one Saturday night. We took on board a second guitarist who didn't really know our stuff and prepared haphazardly for our first and last cheap shot at the dream.

It wasn't that they yelled abuse, that ripe tomatoes or putrid eggs were hurled at the stage, that we played all that badly…we just stunned them

into a prolonged eerie silence. They had never heard the like. I suppose
when an audience is expecting sea shanties and such and they get *You
Made Me Feel Like A Man* and *Heaven Has Claws* you might predict a
riot. We did and got off the stage sharpish heading for the hills of Lees and
Chadderton   post haste.

Not long after the folk club debacle Smartie suggested we make what
would surely be our seminal first album. In the absence of anywhere
resembling a bona fide recording studio his parents' back room became
Abbey Road or, in our case, an unadopted cinder path to nowhere.
The Smarts lived in a cul-de-sac or, in fact, it might have been a sack. I
wouldn't call it dark and dingy but, hey, that's the kind of nice guy that I
am. Still; it was roomy if gloomy and we set up there with our imported
engineer, Nigel, who supplied a neat home-made box of effects tricks that
only he and Smartie remotely understood and, occasionally, got to work.
The whole weekend stretched before us although, with just a couple of
tracks completed, I departed for a driving lesson with BSM in Oldham.
On my return, my hot girlfriend (and eventual lifetime squeeze) had
arrived. Soon, she was exhibiting all the signs of terminal boredom - the
kind that restringing guitars and searching for the lost cord (of my blue
and white stripy pyjamas) might be expected to induce. She took to
drumming on a discarded meat pie in desperation before disappearing like
the morning mist. After she'd gone we decided the meat pie was no longer
fit for human consumption and gave it to Grasper, the Smarts' Standard
Poodle. He took one sniff, looked up at us with haughty disdain and shook

his woolly head before walking away. Clearly, Hollands' best wasn't up to his standard. I often wonder (Liar! But I'm wondering now) what happened to the meat pie.

Sunday morning dawned at the Smarts and we crawled reluctantly out of our sleeping bags blinking like moles dug out of holes to face another day's recording and, in my case, the reality of a paralysed hand. I'd been sleeping on it and now it was a dangling, bloodless extremity unfit for purpose (ie tonking my tambourine). As the prospect of hospital and a bloody, botched amputation loomed into view I frantically shook my paw till, slowly, the red stuff began to fill my fingers and some feeling returned. PHEW!

DRAWING: Simon, horrified at his floppy wrist and pale dangling digits, imagining a mad doc' with an axe wearing a bloodstained white coat hovering near at hand.

We needed the sound of a dog in full voice for our 'Freeport' track and Grasper refused to cooperate. Apparently, he rarely barked and nothing we did, including the copious supply of treats, induced a whimper or a wuff out of him. Reluctantly, Smartie and I tramped the neighbourhood with a small battery-operated tape recorder in search of a co-operative canine. We eventually came across a large bloke with a small dachshund that was straining in mid-dump on some wasteland nearby.

'Does he bark?' said Smartie.

'Usually! Just before he bites,' the man replied. 'And he bites if anyone interrupts his ablutions.'

'What are those?' I enquired.

'When he's havin' a crap,' explained Smartie, already legging it at some speed down the road. I quickly followed in his wake leaving the large bloke laughing fit to bust.

Another track we wanted to put down (probably appropriately) required the sound of a church bell ringing intermittently which presented a problem.

The Smarts' place was marooned in the bleak environs of suburbia and any small churches nearby were not likely to have clangers. Even if they had, would they be willing to ring them for us or accept a pitifully meager bribe so to do. Unlikely, to say the least. Nevertheless, cometh the hour cometh the man - in this case Nige our geeky engineer. He suddenly piped up, taking us by surprise.

'My brother, Fred, works in a brewery.' We looked at him like men in a dream, pondering the relevance of that meaningless remark to the problem of the bell. There seemed no likelihood of imminent enlightenment so Smartie's 'Bollocks!' reply was as good as any, I thought. But Nige wasn't finished with us yet.

'I don't know exactly what he does - he's never been specific - but it's something to do with gravity.' We looked at each other, both completely bewildered.

'He's been at the wacky baccy again,' I speculated.

'Gravity!' exclaimed Smartie. 'What does he do - put on a space suit and float around above the vats sprinkling yeast everywhere?'

'Don't be daft,' I said. 'He wouldn't be sprinkling yeast everywhere. He'd be stirring up the brew with a sterilized spoon after adding a big bag of Tate and Lyle.'

'Yes. You're right, Simon. I can see him now…..Fred the Fermenter, hovering outside his loony vehicle in search of the perfect froth.'

You might not find this funny - Nige certainly didn't - but Smartie and I were in tears, rendered helpless by humour, legless with laughter, tickled pink, nay cerise, at the mind pic' of it all.

'One small stir for man: one big spoonful for mankind,' I somehow managed through the mirth, ballsing up Neil Armstrong's words on the moon like everyone else.

'When you've finished, you two,' barked a narked Nige. 'The thing is he gets a beer allowance every week.'

'SO WHAT!' we yelled together.

'Well, he gets to take it home see…'

'Nige,' pleaded Smartie. 'Get to the sharp end - the bloody point man.'

'The point is he also takes home a carbon dioxide, CO2, cylinder along with the beer.'

'Pity it's not carbon monoxide,' groaned Smartie. 'I'm up for an early death listening to you.'

'Let him finish,' I said. 'The suspense is killing me.'

'CO2 cylinders sound like a bell ringing,' droned Nige. 'Bang the sides with a hammer or whatever and there you are.' Triumphant, he flicked away an unwholesome bogey hanging perilously from his left nostril. It landed on Grasper who was sleeping off his treats in front of the fire - no doubt dreaming of lithesome lady pooches and pies fit for canine consumption.

'Bloody Hell, Nige!' shouted Smartie.

'Serves him right,' muttered Nige. 'Turning his nose up at that meat pie.'

'I didn't mean about the bogey,' said Smartie. 'I mean you're a genius, mate.'

'He is!' I concurred.

'Am I?' queried Nige.

'YES!' we exclaimed, heartily.

Within the hour said Fred arrived with the cylinder which was just the job - well, just the cylinder really - and perfect for our purposes. Pity it was a crap track after all.

Our engineer, Nige, was a quiet lad and his effects contraption liked to emulate its creator, often refusing to function properly if at all. After a prolonged period of almost monkish muteness it suddenly burst into life with a roaring vengeance which would have woken the neighbourhood that Sunday morning but for the fact that Smartie had the headphones plugged in as he listened to a track. Nige's 'concraption' flooded feedback loudly through the cans clamped either side of Smartie's cranium. The electric shock expression on his creased face made us howl.

'Flamin' 'eck, Nige, you moron!' he bellowed. 'You nearly blew me ears off!'

DRAWING: Smartie and his ears, in mid-air, parting company.

There was no immediate response from our preoccupied engineer. Further complaints emanated from my friend in the form of extreme verbal abuse unfit for publication. It was, however, captured on tape in perpetuity and this tirade remains a source of some embarrassment to him even now. Everyone at the Heights has heard it at one time or another and enjoyed a giggle - hardly believing their laid back neighbour capable of such a swearfest.

Needless to say, Smartie blames me for this state of affairs. As they say in the States, I'm taking the Fifth on that one but the recording is one helluvah party piece. As the tape runs out Nige's, admirably restrained, one word reply can just be discerned…'KNICKERS!'.

Being in a band in those halcyon days, even a naff one with no gigs, was a great babe magnet. Locked in the throes of late adolescence, Smartie and I were increasingly on the lookout for likely and lively girls. Or, as he put it somewhat hypocritically, sincere ones. I was ready to fall in love at the drop of a hat or my father's flat cap in the hall cupboard. I confess, I still have a lingering, no doubt rose-tinted, affection for all my exes. Hazey Jane from Lisburn Lane – farther out than the tide at Southport; Maureen, the dramatic, dark- eyed temptress with the prosaic name; Christine, a lady in red long before Chris the Berk came on the scene; Sue from the coffee bar on George Street who had God and good sense on her side;

Julia and Anne - nightingales but, ultimately, distant birds of a feather;
Gillian from Halifax who was looking for a Man but neither of us. And
others too fleeting to mention.

I bullied and cajoled Smartie and engineer Nigel till we had a double el
pea in the bag ready to unleash upon an unsuspecting world. We finally
emerged bleary- eyed, hungry and yawning into the pitiless rain of a
mid-October morning. Having been imprisoned with the Smarts (sounds
like a painful rectal condition) for what seemed like a lifetime, patience
was wearing thin on all sides. That evening in our local, The Whitegate,
over a brown split with bitter I recovered enough to walk my hot girlfriend
back to her place and trek the remaining couple of miles home. Tramping
doggedly along under the yellowing gloom of the streetlights on
Broadway I imagined what car I would get when I passed my driving test.
Visions of maroon Capris, sporty MGs and, ludicrously, a sleek yellow
Lambo' ran through my mind but, strangely, never one of a blue, two-year
old Morris Minor van that needed a new petrol pump. I leave the rest to
your imagination.

CHAPTER SIX: BUSY BODDIES AND HORNYOLOGY

Lately, I have become interested in history - not old kings and queens like
Henry the Eighth and Larry Grayson - but the family, genealogy, sort of
stuff. I never took much interest in either as a kid. Funnily enough,
Smartie seemed to revive his long-standing interest in the subject at much

the same   time so it will come as no surprise to learn that our ultra-glam
neighbour, Clovella Skinley, is well into it. She has traced her lineage
back to Boadicea who was queen of the Iceni tribe and probably the most
famous person from Norfolk outside of Sir Cloudesley Shovell, drowned
Admiral of the Fleet, and Charles 'Turnip' Townsend, inventor of the
four-course crop rotation system. Smartie claims to be a distant
descendant - well, out of sight really - of William the Bastard which just
confirms what many of us suspected all along.

The great and the good in those days of yores (and mine) were invariably
defined by the definite article; hence the Duke of Burgundy was Charles
the Rash. You wouldn't want to be sat next to him at the mediaeval
banqueting table, would you? Impetigo, shingles, bubonic plague or just
an allergic reaction to mouldy mutton or pig's trotters? Who'd want to
risk it? The old Duke was probably a bit of a wild bore himself. Then
there's Edward the Confessor. What was he confessing to or about? He
was the seventh son of Ethelred the Unready (so Ethelred wasn't always
unready when it came to bedroom shenanigans). Going back to William
the Bastard, a very competent conqueror but known to be illiterate, he put
on a lot of weight in later years and ballooned to a gross size. On his
demise, priests tried to stuff his body into a stone coffin at the funeral but
it proved a tad on the small size. The Bastard's corpulent corpse exploded
and bespattered all those in the vicinity, including the priests.
Understandably, they probably uttered his name in vain on that
melancholy (and messy) occasion.

DRAWING: William's remains exploding out of his stone coffin over everyone. The word 'bastard' is being bandied about by all and sundry.

Incidentally, my historical tome states he was the first Norman King of England. But, surely, he was the first William King of England? Besides, you can't have a King Norman any more than a King Cyril or a King Cecil. They'd be laughed out of court. I also came across a weird dude called Pedro the Cruel during my researches. He was reputed to be a mate of William's, possibly a member of his extended family. Pedro the Cruel Bastard, maybe? It must have been awkward at the old medieval banqueting table. If someone wanting the ancient condiments shouted 'Pass me the salt and pepper, yer bastard!' the two bastards wouldn't have known which of them he was talking to.

Clovella's sadly deceased hubby, Septimus, (jeez, Septimus Skinley) had a tax collector in the family, an uncle Pierre, who died of Gaul stones - thrown at him by French peasants who were revolting (and still are for all I know). Awesome. She also had a talented female relative, Edna, who danced at the Moulin Rouge and married a French impressionist related to Alistair McGowan. Impressive indeed.

We called on Clovella one sunny afternoon to check out her family tree, or bush as she thrillingly called it, over Green tea and Garibaldis on the lawn - dunking obligatory. The last time we'd seen her she'd just discovered Edna but her researches seemed to have petered out since. The only new info' concerned Uncle Pierre whose cause of death was, and I quote from the certificate, 'stoned' - a verdict open to misinterpretation by the stupid.

Was cannabis a deadly drug back then in the anals or any other orifice of history? Only Bob Marley's great, great, great, great, great, great grandad knows. Spliffing.

Smartie and I devoured the huge plate of Garibaldis while our sensuous host was busy with the Rosie Lee. Proper leaves she used too. None of your tea bags rubbish. And she'd brought out the best China in our honour. Clovella oozed class you see. I reckon you could have eaten her nail clippings and drunk her bath water she was such a peach. I wondered how I could still feel like that about a woman at my age but I was made up that I could. The only fly in the ointment was my old friend. All being fair in love, war and whist, I determined when I got home to google super-size electrocutors with a three year pest warranty, hoping they made one big enough.

After tea, inside the house, Clovella looked tired and more than a tad weary. It was then that we noticed an old Singer sewing machine and a pile of material under the table in the far corner of the room.

'What's that lot?' enquired Smartie.

'Nothing,' she replied, unconvincingly. 'I'm busy with some curtains.'

'You don't look like you need any,' I said, glancing round the room at her beige, almost new, Japanese-patterned ones over the windows. She looked away sheepishly and we both sensed something was not quite kosher. Smartie was a step ahead of me.

'They're for her aren't they…Betty Boomslanger? Why are you making curtains for The Boom?' Clovella looked ashen and fit to burst into tears.

She could hardly get the words out.

'For Herbert!' she whispered, nodding in the direction of her chic, French-polished sideboard. On top on a lace mat was a large glass bowl of water with a goldfish swimming merrily around giving us the eye. 'My granddaughter, Hannah, bought him as a present for my birthday and…..well, I've got rather used to him now. The warden found out about Herbert and threatened to have him taken away by the RSPCA. Then; she sort of mentioned she needed new curtains and …'

'We can guess the rest,' I said.

'Blackmail!' exclaimed an apoplectic Smartie, The veins in his neck were positively bulging and mine weren't far behind. Clovella, though, had rallied and insisted she didn't mind doing the curtains. It was just that Betty wanted them ready by Saturday - a schedule that would have tested a pro'.

'That Betty, she's a…' I began.

'So and so,' interrupted Clovella.

'Or a sew and sew in this case,' gagged Smartie. We laughed and enjoyed reminiscing together till Smartie and I left a couple of hours later having gorged on the Garibaldis and knowing rather more than we wanted to about Boudicea or Boudica, Queen of the Iceni, and her ancient ruck with the Romans. We passed Betty Boomslanger on her rounds. Her nose was in the air as usual and the corks of her bush hat were swinging wildly in the stiff breeze.

'Let's raise a posse and spike that Aussie,' growled Smartie.

'You said it,' I said. And he had.

DRAWING: An incandescent, apoplectic Smartie, steam emanating from every orifice, choking on a huge Garribaldi.

The next day we were passing Betty's back garden and saw our old friend Harry Butt wielding a spade and turning over the soggy clay soil for all he was worth.

'Watcha, Harry!' yelled Smartie. Exhausted, our old friend leaned on his implement and desperately gulped in air. He looked across at us ruefully, obviously a tad embarrassed.

'What's the score?' I asked him, knowing he was hardly a horny-handed son of the soil. He looked round to make sure we were alone.

'Got me by the short and curlies, hasn't she?' he announced.

'Smoking?' said Smartie.

'What else?' he replied. 'Caught me the other night and threatened to get on to the council.'

'Happened to mention she wanted some labouring done, did she?' Harry nodded.

'See you in The Shamrock for a pint later lads,' he added, thumping the spade into another clump of sodden earth fighting to stay untilled. We walked on in a daze, not knowing the half of it yet.

Within the week, other tales of blackmail and extortion emerged and it seemed like the contagion was spreading rapidly amongst the citizens of Stalag Apfel Heights. Those affected were invariably good at something - often something skilled that would usually require remuneration. Even ninety year-old Daisy Dimmock who'd been an accountant suddenly found herself busy with the books of an outfit called 'Busy Bodies Cleaners', a company she'd never heard of or had any dealings with before. She looked none too pleased about it.

I contacted my trusty grandson, Jack, who found out that the BBC (no, not that one) had two named directors. One was a certain E Boomslanger with an out of date address in Birdsville, Queensland, probably the remotest place on the planet and sandwiched between two deserts. The population amounted to a hundred hapless Aussies and, presumably, a surplus of their feathered friends. Apparently, Birdsville gets just twenty-two days of rain a year - about enough for the kids to fill their water pistols and the birds to have a quick bath and wet their feathers. The other director was one B Boomslanger, Betty's brother Burt. His address, equally out of date, was Brown Street, Bogabilla, on the Queensland and New South Wales border. Bogabilla is described as "a bit of a thriller" due to its amazing creeks. Ominously though, "concern has been expressed as to the health consequences of high levels of violence". So, if you're ever Down Under, best give Bogabilla a miss despite those amazing creeks - you might find yourself up a shit one without the proverbial paddle.

DRAWING: A raging but scenic Bogabilla creek. Floating upside down is a battered canoe having endured a high level of violence. A ghostly paddle, personified, looks down from the Heavens above.

Smartie and I wondered if Betty and Burt really did originate from Birdsville and Bogabilla or had manipulated their genealogical pedigree and locations to make them so unlikely they'd seem to be true. We couldn't decide.

Over the next few weeks we noticed that a lot of familiar faces weren't around during the day. Benches at The Heights were usually at a premium, especially lakeside or in the gardens. If you spotted a vacant one from a distance on a summer's day you made a beeline for it. Often, a hilarious, speed-walking race ensued with the winners throwing themselves ass-first on to a bench inches in front of the competition. The losers usually turned round and walked off trying to appear nonchalant as if they'd no interest in sitting down whatsoever. Then, there was the lack of washing pegged out to dry and nobody in their garden hailing us as we passed by. The Heights is known hereabouts as the land of the living dead but, suddenly, it seemed like an empty zombie park during the day. Undoubtedly something was afoot (or at least nine inches) and Betty and Burt's Busy Boddies company was prime suspect we reckoned. That evening Smartie and I called on Lily Macduff. Everyone else we'd tried had just clammed up but Lily was always outspoken and usually in the know. It was likely she'd be willing to spill the beans if we pressed her hard enough. She was lovely and loveable but notoriously mean. A native of Govan, she was a Scot's girl that had taken the low road to England in her twenties but her accent and her down to earth outlook were ingrained and immutable. As related, even The Boom had come out second best in a fratch match with Lily over a certain library book. Lily had remained undaunted. She would have taken Heinz to court if she'd found only 56 beans in one of their cans.

As we arrived at Lily's house we saw an ambulance with flashing lights pulled up outside. Two paramedics emerged from the front door carrying Lily on a stretcher. She was unconscious and covered in her beloved tartan blanket - a Christmas present from her son, Alastair, who was something in the city. That city being London, he was rarely, if ever, seen 'oop North' at The Heights. The occasional phone call was pretty much their only point of contact. As we looked on helplessly there was no sign of The Boom who should have been there organising things and generally helping out. That night she was a privileged guest at the Mayor's inaugural ball. Her mobile was unaccountably turned off. A sackable offence? Not with Betty's connections. Officialdom put it down to 'an unfortunate oversight - just one of those things' and her name remained in the frame for warden of the year while Lily remained in hospital the rest of the week. The underlying problem was exhaustion but, being diabetic, there were complications. Alistair sent a 'Get Well' card that arrived at the hospital the day after Lily returned to The Heights.

Busy Boddies & Co, temporarily at least, lost a huge chunk of its geriatric workforce and had to employ younger workers on the minimum wage which was a big downer for the Downunderers. Betty and Burt's hold over the oldsters didn't cut it en masse - the council could hardly make them all homeless. After Lily's 'bad do' and Betty's no-show, no one was going cleaning and labouring for the two 'B's anymore, whatever the consequences. Betty fumed and threatened but to no avail. Busy Boddies was a busted flush and rapidly going down the toilet. Leading the defiance as she slowly recovered was Lily Macduff - the Arthur Scargill of The Heights. Just as feisty with a better hairstyle. She wrote to some seemingly honest councillors; the papers; the CBI and our expenses cheat MP, Makin A. Packett, till even Betty's influential friends in high places looked like they couldn't save her from the chop. Incredibly, clinging on by her exquisitely manicured fingernails, she somehow survived.

DRAWING: Oldsters charging ecstatically out of the offices of Busy Boddies *& Co* throwing away their mops and buckets.

A few weeks later Smartie spotted the not unexpected news that Busy Boddies *& Co* was no more. Betty and Burt's attempts to run a legitimate business had proved lamentable. Without virtually free labour on tap its demise had been swift and humiliating accompanied by sordid publicity. Betty had been beaten and she knew it but it was just another battle in a long war of geriatric attrition. Time and a supremely autocratic nature were on her side and she was sure to redouble her efforts to make all our lives as miserable as she could. It was war for sure - but with a few laughs along the way.

The traditional summer fete at Stalag Apfel Heights was usually a fairly tame affair but Smartie, Lily, Clovella and I were dreaming up something different this year. The theme was a Betty and Burt extravaganza and we attracted the locals in great numbers which raised a goodly sum for charity and The Heights' entertainment fund. There was a coconut shy with Betty and Burt figures as targets, a donkey derby with Betty and Burt donkeys and, at the Wacky Races hoop-la, you could win you your very own Creepy Coupe driven by the Aussie 'Gruesome Twosome'. Everyone got an Aussie hat on arrival with Betty cork danglers and a pair of red plastic devil's horns sticking out on top. The side of the hat featured a sticker imprinted with 'SHEILA-DEVIL' in large letters. The stalls were festooned with hundreds of 'Betty' balloons with her picture on them and the legend 'GET HER OUT- BACK HOME!' while a rash of 'NOT WANTED' posters with Betty and Burt pics on them spread everywhere. A huge bewhiskered Betty Boomtown Rat looked down from above the entrance to the community centre with an 'I DON'T LIKE FUN DAYS!' speech bubble. Strangely, the lady herself, and I use that term almost hanging off, was nowhere to be seen.

The History of Things 6

School dinners at the South Chadd sinkhole were pure pigswill. The dinner ladies were all mumsy-looking characters to look at but closet sadists underneath their reassuring exteriors. The self-satisfied smirks on their faces as they dished their latest culinary calamity on to our plates told you as much. They must have been trained by British Rail at the apogee of nasty nosh nationalisation. The proprietors of the worst kind of inner city greasy spoons would have curled up in shame and embarrassment at the slushy sago and wretched rice pud' we were expected to eat. What is sago anyway?

No one had a clue back then. It wouldn't have helped if we'd known it was starch extracted from the pithy insides of tropical palm stems - pretty much bamboo bone marrow and, reputedly, the staple food of the Moluccas. Whoever they are, the Moluccas would probably be better off eating staples. Rolled into balls and mixed with boiling water the goo forms a wallpaper-like paste the taste of which I can unhappily recall some fifty years later.

One particular dinner lady, busty Beryl, lived for Thursdays, sago day, when she could watch us wriggle and squirm. A sago sadist of the first order, Beryl refused to collect a bowl unless it was empty or one of her victims had barfed into it. It was difficult to determine the nature of the contents most of the time. Sago, huh – way to go.

DRAWING: Sago barf fest amongst us school kids in the dining hall.

To avoid Thursday school dinners Smartie and I weren't the only ones who shovelled their mum's lunch loot into the chip shop's coffers. Charlie's Chippy was heaving on Thursdays after midday. On the bell for lunch break it was like the start of the Manchester marathon at the school gates and likewise along the quarter of a mile down Stanley Road (are you listening, Mr Weller?) to Charlie's. A bag of chips or a dab butty and life was worth living again. We usually hung out to devour Charlie's gourmet grub in nearby Coalshaw Green park. Sometimes we'd mill around the newsagent's looking, we thought, nonchalant and cool, our grubby little faces exuding bursting acne and latent angst. Happy days - though that didn't stop us counting them down till the long summer holiday. Six weeks of blissful freedom for us and six weeks getting paid for doing even less than usual for our tormentors. Well; there's always a downside, isn't there?

DRAWING: Charlie's chippy bursting with school kids with acne - their pustules bursting forth.

Smartie had plans for a camping trip one summer. Naturally, I was invited along. Someone had to lug the tent and stuff around from place to place and generally play Man Friday to his Robinson Crusoe. Somehow, I passed the audition. Joining us would be sound engineer Nigel who was a massive Pink Floyd fan and into psychedelic everything. He claimed to be on a mission to 'find himself' in the outback of rural England. Nige was sure there were eccentric English aborigines, probably naked ones, in strange sounding places like Fangfoss and Foggathorpe with bizarre pagan rituals, ancient understanding of what he called the 'rural universe' and magic mushrooms aplenty. Like his box of sound effects, Nige's brain only worked intermittently- usually coinciding with uncomfortable collisions with reality.

Smartie was our leader - self-appointed, of course - in charge of planning our route through whatever part of the country he decided we should explore. It turned out to be the North and East Ridings of Yorkshire. I asked him why he'd plumped for Tykedom. Was it good camping sites and bus connections; a favourable weather forecast for the area; flat countryside as we'd be on Shanks's pony a lot of the time; exciting places to visit in the vicinity or, perhaps, chocolate-box village locations?

'None of them,' he announced.

'Well, what then?' I responded, fairly taken aback.

'Birds!' he exclaimed, managing to be both mysterious and belligerent at the same time.

'Birds! What's with birds? Since when have you been interested in hornyology?'

'I suppose you mean ornithology,' he replied in his snooty, Prince Charles accent.

'Whatever!' Smartie sniggered, teetering on the brink of a guffaw. Sometimes he got further up my nose than a blind earwig and I told him so.

'Simon. Get back in your kennel and zip it, there's a good boy. If you must know, I've discovered through painstaking and meticulous research that Yorkshire contains more eligible, unattached crumpet than anywhere else in Britain. Clackmannanshire in Scotland runs it close but unless you fancy a long trip and a Highland fling Yorkshire it is. Savvy?'

Personally, I would have preferred Devon. It was warmer with cute coves and clotted cream teas. Nige' expressed a yearning to visit the land of his fathers - apparently he had two - in Wales. Smartie would have none of it (though he hoped for a helping or two along the way) and brushed aside all arguments to the contrary. Due to his, admittedly understandable, liking for the lasses and, less so, his gran's Yorkshire puds, the land of cricket and abundant crumpet beckoned. I'd been right all along - it was down to 'hornyology' after all.

Smartie, as befits his nomenclature, was a clever lad but, occasionally, something went wrong and he turned out to be as bright as a two-watt bulb. His travel itinerary was a shambles. We set off by slow train from Manchester and found ourselves stranded at the deserted bus station of a small Yorkshire town at five o'clock in the morning waiting for the 5B to Bishop's Burton. It was due at quarter to nine.

'Form an orderly queue men,' barked our Great Leader, laughing the whole thing off. What none of us could laugh off in our lightweight summer togs was the drizzle and cold though Nige took it in his stride and walked off to look in shop windows to pass the time. Smartie mined and flicked away bogies in that disgusting way he had while I…….don't remember what I did. I know what I'd like to have done but there was nowhere to bury the body in that concrete jungle which saved Smartie's ass.

A dirty white Transit van arrived and a scruffy, bleary-eyed bloke dropped a pile of morning papers outside the newsagent's shop. Writ large on the side of the van was 'WASH ME!' Passing by and seeming to notice it for the first time, the bloke stopped in his tracks and added, 'WASH YOURSELF!?' in a decidedly shaky hand. Parky's or Delirium Tremens? My guess was the DTs.

'That bloke drove off in a huff,' mused Smartie.

'Really?' I said. 'It looked more like a Transit van to me.' Silence ensued till the arrival of our bus…almost four hours later.

DRAWING: A bogie-flicking Smartie and I watching the wreck of a bloke writing with a trembling hand on the side of his dirty van, advanced workman's bottom on show.

The 5B dropped us off before Bishop's Burton near a busy campsite. Unfortunately, it was the wrong campsite - another Smartie slip up. A two and a half mile trek later we arrived at the right site, near the quiet little village of Wipers Bottom, where we found a suitably scenic spot to put up Smartie's tent.

'Ever put up a tent you guys?' he enquired.

'I know you put one up with guys. And loads of pegs,' I recalled. Otherwise, blank looks from Nige and me. Both of us knew perfectly well how to put up a tent but Nige was occupied dodging a determined wasp attracted, it seemed, by an Uncle Joe's mint ball he was sucking and I was determined that Smartie, for once, was going to do most of the work. I figured he deserved to. When, at last, he was finished it looked okay if a tad on the small side for the three of us.

'That's a two-man tent, isn't it?' queried Nige.

'Yep!' announced Smartie, 'but we can fit you in as well.' Nige looked puzzled and wandered off to look at some cows in the next field.

'You asswipe!' I said to Smartie, feeling distinctly peeved. 'You told us your cousin Angus and his family of five used it for holidays.'

'He does. They do. It's used to store equipment by the side of the big tent.'

'How are three of us going to fit in there?' I fumed. That first night, under a full moon, I found out. Smartie and Nige faced one way either side of me. I was piggy in the middle facing the tent flap. Their feet, even inside sleeping bags, smelt of rancid Stilton and Nige mentioned he had Athlete's Foot for good measure. I stuffed pieces of kitchen roll up my nostrils and nearly suffocated till morning.

DRAWING: Of inside the cramped tent. Odours are depicted emanating from Smartie and Nige's feet curling a convoluted path through the dank atmosphere towards my nose. I am wide awake and gritting my teeth.

I had no intention of making brecky next morning but Smartie and Nige's foot rot together with urgently needing a pee forced me to scramble over them and out of tent Hell around 6am. I think my knee landed in Smartie's eye at some point but he didn't wake up. It was cold and I left the zip open on the tent flap hoping they'd both get frostbite. Later, with my crutch feeling decidedly numb, I realised I'd left the zip of my trousers open too. I was lucky icicles hadn't formed and thoughts of gangrene and penile amputation chilled me to the bone.

Bacon and sausages were sizzling on the camping stove when the others finally emerged into daylight. I have to say that bacon butties never tasted so good before or after that day. Perhaps it was the fresh air or some sort of Elvish magic but those butts washed down with mugs of steaming hot tea remain unsurpassed in my ongoing gastronomical history.

'Psychedelic!' exclaimed Nige, pausing in mid-munch. 'These are far out, man. I can tell you guys, these beauties are setting the controls for the heart of the sun. Wow!'

After our psychedelic breakfast, a la Floyd and Alan, we wandered around and came across the rotting hulk of a small, post-Beeching railway station outside the village - now just a stain on Wipers Bottom after a hundred years as the hub of the community. The track hadn't been taken up and we decided, for no particular reason, to walk along it to the next station. There are two things that you really don't want to happen in that situation, one being the sudden realisation that, despite the station being closed, the line is still in use- emphasised by the York express baring down on you almost before you know it. The other thing is getting caught short along the way. We got lucky regarding the line and the express but, suddenly, Smartie stopped, literally, in his tracks.

'Hey, guys. You head on. I'll catch you up.'

'Fagged out?' I asked him. 'We can rest here a while.'

'No…it's cool. You guys carry on. Don't mind me.' Nige and I leaned on a gate into a cornfield and he switched on the small transistor radio he'd brought along, invariably tuned into the pirate music station Radio Caroline. It was the home in those days of great DJs like John Peel together with a few muppets who shall remain shameless. Procul Harum's classic, *A Whiter Shade Of Pale*, issued forth soothing our fevered brows (I had the remnants of Asian 'flu) and those of the creatures of field and hedgerow. All except Smartie whose ghastly face emulated the aspect of the song title. Clearly, something was 'up'. I thought at first it might be his breakfast which, like myself on myriad occasions, hadn't agreed with him. It transpired I was at the wrong end of a stick no one would want to get hold of.

'Will you two bozos bugger off,' demanded Smartie, almost dancing. His face was creased in obvious but highly entertaining discomfort. By then, Nige and I had twigged. Sad to relate, in our view, Smartie's bad luck simply added to the joys of existence and we decided to let him squirm awhile.

'Got a fag?' I asked Nige, casually.

'No. But I'd love one,' he replied.

'Neither of you bastards smoke,' yelled Smartie, bent over, gritting his teeth and hopping from one leg to the other trying to ward off imminent disaster. We looked at him blankly.

'Anything wrong?' we chimed together. Smartie paused to pick up several large chunks of ballast to throw at us but we legged it laughing before he could. From a safe distance we stopped and turned to see him fairly dancing a jig. Our mutual friend (Dickensian echoes there) was in a dilemma. The landscape was flat and there was nowhere to hide. He was visible from the country road running parallel nearby and any number of farmers' fields round and about. He might have squeezed behind a telegraph pole but partial exposure would still have been a problem. If only we'd been there a few years later when riotous shrubs, saplings and brambles would have provided plenty of cover where, now, only infant weeds abounded. It was then that Smartie's eyes focused on an object that offered some hope if not expectation - a Wipers Bottom Rural District

Council grit box by the side of the line. Large, concrete and rectangular with a hinged wooden lid, it would suffice if empty. Being summer it was - though not for long.

Smartie waved us further away and we were happy to oblige. Turning, we observed his hapless little figure perched precariously on top of the grit box with the heavy wooden lid resting painfully across his shoulders and back. An old crow sitting on a fence looked on, fascinated by the spectacle, and a phalanx of flies gathered above him in anticipation. All around an eerie silence fell upon the land.

Laughing, Nige and I set off walking towards the promised land of Fangfoss where he was destined to be sadly disappointed. The nearest thing to a pagan ritual was the postman delivering letters to some cottages and his 'rural universe' amounted to the old station, a phone box and not much else. A little later Smartie arrived and gave us the dirtiest (appropriately) of dirty looks. He continued to be in a foul (equally appropriately) mood for the rest of the day and refused to walk back along the track - leaving us to dodge the odd passing car and dive into a ditch when a tractor trundled by on the narrow country road. Adjacent to his open grit box, Smartie averted his eyes towards the tarmac but the object held a strange, almost mystical, fascination for me and Nige. The old crow was nowhere to be seen having probably fallen from its perch after a heart attack. Unsurprisingly, several hundred more flies had joined the party after the pooper had left. Nige and I shook our heads and smirked surreptitiously - wondering why Smartie hadn't shut the lid.

DRAWING: A straining Smartie perched on the grit box trackside with an old crow on a fence giving him the eye and, somehow depicted, an eerie silence descending from above.

'What do you think?' queried Smartie.

'Dodgy!' I exclaimed.

'We could front it out, I reckon.'

'Nah,' said Nige. 'You could, but we couldn't.' Smartie bridled. (gone all equine there)

 But Nige, you're growing a beard,' he pointed out.

'Call that a beard?' I interrupted. 'It's bum fluff!'

'Maybe,' said Smartie, 'but the bottom line is we've nothing to lose.' I couldn't argue with that as my friend knew all about bottoms and lines. So, around seven o'clock that evening it was agreed we'd attempt to pass ourselves off as eighteen year-olds and order three pints of ale in the oddly named Barmaid's Arms, a pub down the road from our coastal campsite. That morning, we had left Wipers Bottom behind. Regrettably, I have to say, as its endless opportunities for cheap toilet humour might have fuelled a few more pages of 'Codger' and saved me from having to think of new stuff.

We had headed for the seaside and Deadcrab Cove which was actually bigger (and livelier) than it sounds. For one thing, it had its own pub which was a huge plus point on our adolescent agenda. And the views from our campsite were to die for - if the drop from the cliff edge was anything to go by. Evening meal was a problem though as the local shop had shut long before we arrived and we were hungry as caterpillars crawling desperately among abundant foliage with their mouths firmly stuck together after their digestive juices had dried out and formed a glue-like bond between their jaws during a prolonged, nay disproportionate, period of inexplicable inactivity. Phew!

(I'm gonna do another one of those later - thoroughly enjoyed it).

Seven pm arrived on time (though my wonky watch still insisted it was 10.17 as usual) and we headed out to the Barmaid's Arms on Huggingham Road in the village. It's rather lukewarmly disputed whether Deadcrab Cove is in fact a village or not. Cigar smokers to a man would call it a hamlet but, personally, I couldn't give a stuff either way.

We sat down at an ill-lit table inside well away from the locals - mostly fishermen who liked beer - and sent Nige to try it on at the bar. The landlord, Jasper Muldoon according to the sign above our heads as we came in, moseyed over to confront an obviously nervy Nige.

'Three pints of your best bitter,' yapped our engineer, adding 'please' rather lamely. The big bearded landlord looked him up and down.

'I can't serve you lad,' he boomed. Immediately, our hearts sank. This didn't look good. Then; Jasper stepped back and revealed his right arm was in a sling. 'I've just got back from the horspital (equines again). I'll get Amber over. She'll see you all right.' A gorgeous, raven-haired beauty appeared from nowhere and pulled our pints so incredibly erotically that I dream of her, occasionally rather damply, to this day. At that moment, in that place, the three of us were love-struck, our eyes bulging out of their sockets and our hormones all of a quiver. Nige returned to our table with the beers. He was shaking all over (a tribute to the awesome Johnny Kidd and The Pirates) and our glasses were almost half empty.

'Amber nectar!' he whispered, his voice trailing off into the ether. None of us touched what was left of our ale. We just sat there in sensual worlds of our own.

'Do you reckon she's the landlord's daughter?' I mused.

'Looking at her…and I still am,' began Smartie, 'and looking at old Jasper… I'd be sus' about the milkman!' he concluded.

The pub hadn't much in the way of food on but we ordered three giant pasties and a spare-tyre-sized bowl of chips which arrived in no time (well, 10.17 according to my watch). They looked like they'd been hanging around a while but we would have eaten a horse (groan) and the pasties, washed down with fine Yorkshire ale, filled yawning craters in our stomachs. We were in two minds - Nige's dysfunctional one being temporarily out of action - as to whether we should try it on again for another round. On the one hand it would be better not to push our luck and, on the other, Amber might serve us. It was a difficult one. The presence of a gnarled old geezer, probably Jasper's grumpy grandad, behind the bar and Amber's continued absence eventually saw us slink out of the door unobserved but still quietly triumphant.

We emerged from the pub into a still, silent, star-lit evening that drew us inexorably towards the Cove and the sandy beach below. We had it to ourselves and strolled along the deserted shoreline under a full moon.

Thoughts of an amorous Amber permeated my adolescent mind…..running my fingers ever so slowly through that long mane of dark hair; kissing those text-book full, red, salt spray lips; reciting Cohen's *Suzanne* to her by pale moonlight and changing the name of his princess; blissfully exchanging promises of undying love and, in my case, slagging off Smartie and Nige, explaining just how unworthy they were of her. Then; Nige started singing….'The way you kiss will always be a very special thing to me,' from Syd Barrett's *Late Night.* That started Smartie off…..'I can't get no satisfaction,' he trilled, ineffably lowering the tone. Obviously, in his primal fashion Smartie shared our attraction to Amber which manifested itself in the lyrics of the old Stones number. It made me wonder for the umpteenth time why I seemed to be under his spell, generally followed where he led, put up with his put downs and somehow remained friends with him whilst perpetually playing second fiddle - a situation that pretty much lasted a lifetime. In many ways I reckon I'm smarter than Smartie but self belief has never been my strong point and, admittedly, I am lazy - my besetting lifelong sin, damn it.

'Let's go swimming,' suggested our great leader and jettisoned his 'Ban the Bomb' t-shirt before running through the rippling surf and diving into the velvet ocean. Nige and I hesitated, looking dubiously at one another, before following suit.

The North Sea, even in August, was still chillsome but we romped around merrily till exhaustion finally overtook us. My teeth chattered on the way back to the campsite and I seemed to have swallowed several saltwater smoothies back at the Cove but I consoled myself that thoughts of Amber would comfort me through the long, smelly night that lay ahead.

DRAWING: Amber pulling our pints in the pub. Our eyes are glazed over observing the spectacle. Jasper Muldoon is sifting and detaching litter and insects from his thick beard with his 'good' arm while grandad Jasper is busy making a ship-in-a-bottle.

CHAPTER SEVEN:

A FOLLOWING WIND AND PSYCHEDELIC WATER

Despite Betty Boomslanger's best attentions the lively residents of Stalag Apfel Heights like to have a good laugh. Whenever she's not in it, the community room frequently echoes to prolonged bouts of mirth which annoys The Boom no end. A competition organised by Smartie particularly aggravates Her Aussieness but remains popular with the rezis. Smartie's 'Fart of the Fortnight' is a blast. Betty disapproved, of course, the moment she got wind of it. She tried her damnedest to stop Smartie in his tracks which brought back to him unhappy memories of hot summers, derelict railway lines, concrete grit boxes and urgent calls of nature. All to no avail. The first 'Fart' was a rip-roaring success with both audience and competitors fairly weeping with laughter. There were short, sharp, explosive ones, medium-length musical ones and long, lingering snorters - all recorded on digital voice recorders supplied by Smartie who transferred the material to computer. His set-up produced amazing CD quality sound. Really, it was all the fun of the fart without the malodorous consequences experienced all too often by the contestants in the privacy of their recording chambers. Smartie defended his concept in front of a Council committee saying it was simply a case of oldies letting off steam (or just letting off). They took the point and failed miserably to find a reason to ban raspberry blowing at The Heights much to Betty's chagrin. Smartie sprang a surprise at the following 'fartfest'. After a good, if not clean, contest the announcement of a winner was delayed. He took the mic' and informed us that a new award for the most musical entry had been decided and hit the play button with aplomb (more likely a finger, methinks). It was a relatively quiet piece of controlled trumping that emulated the melody of an old Jimi Hendrix number - *The Wind Cries Mary*. Lord knows what Mary, or Hendrix for that matter, would have made of it but most of The Heights' rezis didn't catch on and looked distinctly nonplussed. Then, in an outrageous act of self-aggrandizement and being the only competitor in the category, Smartie declared himself the winner. The resounding chorus of boos and jeers consigned the most musical category to Heights' history thereafter. An unrepentant, nay indignant, Smartie hastily announced the winner of 'Fart of the Fortnight'. It was 76 year old Arthur Splurge who'd been a butcher and strongly believed in reincarnation - often regaling us with tales of the dog's life he'd led during the blitz in London. Arthur was sure he'd come back as a ghost which was something of a contradiction as, if it happened, he wouldn't really have come back at all. His entry had been of the rip-roaring variety that took paint off walls, soured fruit and blew spiders off their webs. A worthy winner indeed then.

Everyone was drinking up and about to leave when, unexpectedly, Smartie piped up again.

'Ladies and gentlemen. There's one more piece of business, a FOTF special never to be repeated…not in public anyway. Straight from the bowels of Beelzebub's handmaiden and obtained at great personal risk, I give you the windbreak of all time.'

'Get on with it,' yelled Lily Macduff.

My friend had miraculously managed to record Betty Boomslanger making an involuntary contribution to the competition. When they caught on, the room rocked with laughter before lapsing into silent, pin-drop anticipation. What followed, however, barely troubled the hearing aids. A peevish squeak even a tired mouse would have disowned struggled to rent the air followed by the whispered whoosh of a sickly summer breeze. A groan of acute disappointment greeted Betty's effort - a punctured fart if ever there was one. Happily, the laughter resumed as tea and cakes were ferried in by the Heights' army of volunteers. The Sunday sing-song followed featuring, as usual, *Always Look On The Bright Side Of Life.* Smartie once tried to slip in *My Generation* by The Who but, somehow, "Hope I die before I get old" never endeared itself to the rezis. That day though, my friend redeemed himself with his choice of film for the evening - *Gone With The Wind* - as perspicacious readers will no doubt have anticipated. All this and The Boom out for the evening with her tame councillors. Sometimes, even at Stalag Apfel Heights, life was a gas.

Arthur Splurge, sad to say, was something of a gargoyle. Even Arthur's best friends wouldn't have hailed him as handsome. Nature had not been kind to him. He was tall, rangy and slim which were all to the good but his face and features seemed to have been moulded by a particularly mischievous toddler high on honey and cornflakes. Arthur was a champion gurner though and he had a head start as it were. It required little effort on his part to walk away with first prize almost every time. He had 'gone over the top' on the Somme during the first world war and survived. They say every bullet has its billet but any heading for Arthur would have swerved, in sympathy, elsewhere. None of this mattered because he was a nice guy and popular with everyone - even Betty Boomslanger who seemed strangely attracted to him.

DRAWING: Of the Stalag Apfel Heights fartfest.

A few days after the fartfest Arthur Splurge mysteriously disappeared. Clovella had gone round to his place as arranged for afternoon tea and couldn't get an answer. She was provisionally ghosting *The Splurge Memoirs* which they both hoped would be a bestseller one day detailing Arthur's wartime experiences. When she tried his phone it was dead and, on the basis that Arthur was too, Clovella got the warden to go into the house and check that he was all right…No Arthur. It was a puzzle and shocked the whole community. On day two of his disappearance The Boom reluctantly agreed to report him as a missing person to plod who were too busy manipulating crime figures in their favour to take much interest. Consequently, search parties of all able-bodied oldsters were organised and 'Where Is Arthur' posters flooded the area.

'I wonder what HE would have done?' said Smartie, over a pint in The Shamrock.

'Arthur?'

'No. Sherlock Holmes, you putz!' I was reading the 'What's On' column in the local rag that they keep on the bar when Smartie piped up.

'This would have been right up Holmes's street.' he continued.

'But Arthur was a butcher not a baker,' I pointed out, mischievously.

'There's a time and a place for your pawky humour, Simon, but this isn't it. Be serious.'

'Certainly! But, seriously, it's your round. And it doesn't get more serious than that, matey.'

'What do you reckon's happened to old Arthur then?'

'I haven't a clue,' I replied. 'And neither have you.'

'Clovella's been ringing round the hospitals but they've had no Splurges on the wards.'

'Glad to hear it,' I said. 'She'd do better ringing round the pubs. Arthur liked a pint and a night on the tiles.'

'Yes…but three nights? I suppose he might have run into an old friend.'

'He doesn't drive.'

'Lost his memory then?'

'Forget it!'

'Met an old flame? Joined the circus? Been abducted by little green men from Mars with no sense of smell and a penchant for sticky chocolate bars?' I shook my head.

'Any more likely scenarios occur to you, Sherlock?' He had to admit defeat. But then, so did I. Like everyone else, including plod, we were flummoxed. Unlike plod, we were determined, however unsavoury, to get to the bottom of Arthur's sudden, unaccountable disappearance. Nothing, aside from old age; illness; accident; injury; incontinence; Ebola; cramp attacks; a third round Bananas cup tie against Liverpool; a night at the opera (preferably 'The Phantom Of'); a bad back tweaked putting on a sock; an emergency appendectomy; queuing in the chip shop for second-class stamps thinking it was the post office; queuing in the post office for cod, chips and mushy peas; raging against the iniquity of has-been celebrities endorsing rip-off funeral insurance plans on TV; pin pricking a finger to test blood glucose levels in an ultimately hopeless attempt to forestall diabetic Armageddon; answering an email from a chip shop Elvis or, worse still, that gloomy git Will Self; staying in to wash what's left of our hair; was going to stop us.

DRAWING: 'Sherlock' Smartie sitting at a table in the pub dressed in a long coat and sporting an appropriate pipe but hatless. Above his head is an oil painting of a deer being stalked by a hunter.

Two more Heights oldsters went AWOL soon after Arthur and it seemed like Victorian London and Sherlock Holmes had been left behind in favour of the X Files. Smartie turned into Mouldy but I drew the line at

Skullcap and refused to adopt an American accent, never mind wear women's clothes (as I've always preferred them out of them). I just don't have the legs for it. He tried to persuade me that it was okay, just for a laugh, but I knew who would be laughing. My mind, not my face, was made up and that was that - though I did grow my hair marginally longer and mostly stopped biting my nails.

Assuming his Mouldy role in The Shamrock, Smartie started up again.

'Three of them now - Arthur Splurge, Stanley Pant and Edith Clodgy. What do they have in common?'

'They've all disappeared,' I mused.

'Sometimes I wonder about you, Simon. Besides that?'

'They're all old,' I ventured.

'I'm still wondering about you.'

'All right.....what about the fact that they've all won Fart of the Fortnight at one time or another?'

'Still wondering,' said an exasperated Smartie, in utter disgust. 'You're as much use as a lift in a bungalow. Sup up and shut up!' Grinning, I was happy to comply. Smartie, however, failed to follow his own advice.

'Plod seems to have washed their hands of it. Mind you, they never dirtied them in the first place. It's another case of "You're old and you don't count".'

' That's a bit unfair,' I countered. 'They've got no leads.'

'No dogs either it seems. There should be sniffer dogs on the trail everywhere (memories of geography class and Riggers flooded my mind). We've seen one policeman, that donkey PC Bray, and one scraggy

Alsatian - with a cold. It's not good enough. I'm going to find Arthur and Co, I swear.'

'Stanley Pant will be swearing, wherever he is: he's got Tourette's something shocking. Even The Boom gets red cheeks after a visit to Stan. He called me something unprintable the other day.'

'What?'

'Never mind.'

'Come on, Simon. You've a bounden duty to your readers, if any, to tell us.'

'It was unprintable because I've never heard it before and I don't know how to spell it.'

'Wow! That bad, eh?' I gave Smartie a dirty look instead of the dirty word he was hoping for before supping up and leaving for home. He was left alone in the pub to ponder (a word I really dig - like divot).

The next day after her early morning rounds Betty Boomslanger swanned off on 'urgent business' as she called it. It couldn't be Busy Boddies business - we'd seen to that - but I was wondering what it was when a knock at the door interrupted my thoughts. It was Smartie, of course.

'I've got it!' he announced, triumphantly.

'Well, don't give it me,' I told him, trying to shut the door. It jammed on his outstretched foot and he pushed through, bowling me over in the process. I banged my head hard on the bannister as I overbalanced.

'You...'

'Now, Simon. None of Stanley's stuff, if you please.'

'PRAT!' I bellowed, showing admirable restraint I think.

'It was Edith Clodgy that gave me the idea.'

'She's been found then?'

'No. It was thinking about her, you numpty.' Smartie's theory centred around what Arthur, Stanley and Edith had in common, something I'd pooh- poohed in the pub the night before. He'd concluded that they were all exceptional in some respect. Admittedly, there was Arthur's gurning and Stanley's swearing but I couldn't recall anything exceptional about Edith.

'You don't get it, do you?' crowed Smartie, that smug, supercilious, gloating expression I'd known since schooldays illuminating his face.

'Edith's a medium,' he rattled on. 'She hosts seances in her front room, doesn't she? The Boom was out to ban them, remember, till Edith put her in touch with her late Uncle Seamus from one of those Aussie towns beginning with 'B' - Bastardsville or Bollockstown or something. He told her she'd come into money and marry a Count.'

'Dracula, maybe. By the way, are you sure he said Count?'

'Whatever. The next week Betty won two hundred quid at the Bingo and, suddenly, Edith was in The Boom's good books.'

'What's all this got to do with Betty Boomslanger?' I enquired. Smartie got deadly serious or seriously stupid - I never knew which - and clamped his lips together.

'I don't know - yet. We're going to follow her and find out.' His lips never moved when he spoke and I reckon he would have made a brilliant ventriloquist. All he needed was a dummy. Then, I realised, maybe he had one already.

DRAWING: Edith's seance with The Boom. Uncle Seamus wearing a bush hat and khaki shorts is coming through, a ball and chain round his leg. A sign in the background reads 'Bollockstown Gaol'. A shop nearby is selling 'roo and chips to a queue of fat outbackers. Dracula is around somewhere - his book, *Blood Transfusions for Dummies,* in hand.

The day dawned warm and bright when Smartie and I trailed The Boom to her lair. My old silver Toyota Corolla trundled gamely along behind her sporty red Mazda at a safe distance to avoid recognition. We were heading West towards the coast, painfully aware we'd forgotten to pack our bucket and spades. It soon became obvious as we spotted the tower on the horizon that Betty's 'urgent business' was in Blackpool or somewhere near it. I don't know who was more shocked and surprised - me and Smartie or the startled plod she nearly ran down on Squires Gate Lane. He shook his fist at her and noted her reg'. A good start then and, maybe, an attempted murder charge to follow. We lost her on Devonshire Road but, if a horn was honking anywhere in the vicinity, we knew it would be Betty's and we picked up the trail again effortlessly.

'She's headed for the Prom,' predicted Smartie and it turned out his guess was good. We watched her pull into a narrow private drive and walk along towards a small block of shops with garish names above them. I stopped and let Smartie out to keep an eye on Her Aussieness while I found somewhere to park. Forty minutes later, I met up with him again.

'Where is she?' I burbled, breathlessly. He pointed to a shop front with the most garish sign of them all. It read…..'Betty's Olde Worlde Bazaar of Boobies' which conjured up salacious images of page 3 girls and female talent show judges in provocative states of undress for the delectation of passing punters. Then; I saw the poster depicting weirdy oldsters fit to rival 'Ripley's Believe It or Not' along the way. Framed in the office window above was the unmistakable figure of Betty Boomslanger talking to brother Burt. The gruesome twosome were at it again and had rolled, like two proverbial bad pennies, into Blackpool and along the Golden Mile.

DRAWING: Betty almost running down plod on her way to 'Boobies'.

'What do we do now?' I wondered.

'Buy a couple of silly hats and Cybermen masks. We're going in.'

'Hang on, Smartie. What if they recognise us? It's not much of a disguise.'

'They'll probably kidnap - well, old nap - us and then exhibit us.'

Suitably assured and kitted out, I paid a spotty youth on the door an extortionate tenner and we entered Betty's bizarre bazaar. Inside, it was done up like a series of grotty, grim dungeons along an artificially web-strewn corridor. Each one featured an 'exhibit', three of which were our trio of missing oldsters. Arthur Splurge, grinning and gurning like a good 'un whenever a punter approached, was third in line.

'Arthur!' whispered Smartie, sort of loudly. Our friend paused momentarily but seemed bewildered.

'It's us…Simon and me.' We took off our masks and enlightenment dawned for Arthur.

'What are you doing here?' I asked him, stupidly.

'I should have thought that was obvious,' he replied.

'We thought you'd run off and joined the Foreign Legion,' said Smartie.

'Would have,' began Arthur, 'but for that Legionnaires' disease. And I can't stand sand in my sandwiches…why aren't they called meatwiches or cheesewiches or whatever, I'd like to know.'

'Are you all prisoners here? I asked him, getting down to brass tacks as some oddball people say.

'Not on your Nellie!' rejoined Arthur, laughing.

'Or your Arthur, Stanley and Edith?' queried Smartie.

'No…not on us either.'

'Blimey!' breathed Smartie, pegging his beaky nose between a forefinger and thumb. Arthur looked sheepish.

'Sorry, boys. That was a Houdini - escaped swift and silent like.'

'And deadly,' I added, pegging my own snozzle.

It turned out our three oldsters were on a modest little earner, dressing up and putting on a show - groaning and gurning, swearing like a trooper and telling fortunes in the guise of an old gypsy crone - in Betty and Burt's bazaar. They stayed free of charge at a modest minus one star hotel nearby while they were in town and got to boogie at night in the pubs on the prom.

'What more could you ask for?' said Arthur. Medication, regular meals and emergency alarms occurred to me amongst other things but the three

of them were determined to see out the six weeks contracts they'd signed

and trouser some much needed cash to supplement their meagre pensions.

Like most oldsters, just food, heating and rent took most of their income.

Betty Boomslanger was exploiting them, of course, but the small amount

of extra cash and the delights of the relatively exotic location made it

worthwhile it seemed.

'It's not on, Arthur. Pack it in and come home,' urged Smartie. Arthur

sighed.

'The Heights is all right,' he mused, thoughtfully. 'But it's not home -

never will be. You understand?' We nodded. 'I'm not in a hurry to get

back,' he continued. 'And neither are Stan and Edith. This is…well, fun.

But thanks for thinking of us boys.' We shook old Arthur's hand and left.

'I guess that's it,' I muttered, as we stepped outside into a blast of fresh air

tainted by the sweet smell of candyfloss.

'Nothing we can do,' said Smartie. 'Let's head back ho…back to The

Heights.' Neither of us looked up. If we had, we'd have seen Betty stood

at the window, a wide sardonic grin on her face - only matched by Burt's

alongside her.

DRAWING: Arthur Splurge taking a shower in the desert. A plate of

sandwiches are on a table nearby being eaten by bugs wearing Foreign

Legionnaires' hats.

The History of Things 7

All was still and deeply dark at 3am in the morning following our night at the pub and a dip in the North Sea. I was wide awake and feeling a tad uneasy. A pint, a large pastie and plunging recklessly into the briny suddenly seemed three 'P's too far. Furthermore, on the subject of pees, I had urgent need of one. At the non-flap end of the tent with Smartie, snoring, on one side and Nige, with restless feet syndrome, kicking out (and me) on the other there was nothing for it but to clamber over them and try not to interrupt their erotic dreams of Amber. Then, I thought, sod it! Waking them would serve them right for lusting after MY girl. As I scrambled heedlessly over them and finally reached the tent flap the big toe of my left foot suddenly felt unduly warm and moist. The realisation that it had inadvertently burrowed into Smartie's nostril nearly made me heave. I gingerly removed the offending digit and wiped it on his 'Superman' sleeping bag before opening the zip and diving head first out of the tent - into a cow pat. Luckily, it was a largely dried out one. Things could therefore have been worse, though I didn't think so at the time. My subsequent pee by a tree relieved the immediate situation (and myself) but, as the steam drifted upwards under moonlight, I began to experience tummy turbulence. The nastie pastie from the pub was making its continued presence and stubborn resistance to digestive juices known. Swallowing some salty seawater during our swim at the Cove wasn't exactly helping either. Shivering and sweating, I felt a light drizzle beginning to fall and soak me from head to foot. All this was bad enough but it was the thought of returning to the tent and Smartie and Nige's sweaty feet that took me over the edge. I won't dwell on just how bad I felt - sympathy, I know, will be scant.

Suffice to say, a lifetime ban on beer and pastry (that would have lasted 48 hours at most) passed through my mind as, finally, I tottered back to the tent to face my friends' feet again. Needless to say, they were awake.

'Simon. Is that you?'

'What's up?'

'Almost everything,' I replied, before tramping all over them and collapsing in a pitiful heap. It was then that Smartie howled fit to wake the campsite. His hand had located the snot smear my big toe had left behind on his sleeping bag.

DRAWING: Tent Hell! The big toe and nostril episode.

We moved on shortly afterwards leaving Deadcrab Cove and Amber regretfully behind (though her gorgeous behind was haunting all our dreams).   I thought I'd never see her again but it so happens that, eventually, I did. So; make some noise for a second book, guys.

We took several buses (and never gave them back) then got a lift in a farmer's truck to our next destination - the quaint Dales village of Retchington Hugeley which nestled neatly, if somewhat inconveniently, off the beaten track (Ouch!). As we discovered, Retchington was in fact the smallest of three Hugeleys, the others being Nether Hugeley and Crappington Hugeley - the latter a town complete with all a town's amenities but rather spoiled, or should that be soiled, by the presence of a large sewage works on the outskirts. In contrast, Retchington was chocolate box pretty and had a grand stately home on the doorstep which was said to have belonged to the Duke of Wellington. Well; he stayed there overnight once and had dinner to boot.

We set up the tent and Smartie and Nige set off on a walk while I pretended to be busy round the camp. As soon as they were out of sight I was lounging with a beer in hand and a Consulate between my lips. Consulates were menthol and mental ciggies. Who would want a menthol fag? The concept is utterly flawed but, like you do at that age, I occasionally bought a pack and thought I looked cool smoking them. When they got back, Nige challenged me to a smoking contest while Smartie went off in search of another grit box or the campsite equivalent. I reckon he'd got a taste, if that's the right word (and I know it isn't), for perching during dumping even if you came away with deep indentations across the back of your legs.

Nige and I got through a pack of ten Park Drive each - no mean feat - and were on our eleventh when Nige ran off in search of Smartie looking distinctly pale and wan. I still felt okay though I was glad enough the contest was over. I suppose I cheated really as I never inhaled, taking a drag and blowing the smoke straight out again. If he noticed, Nige never complained. Over the years I've bought the odd packet of fags and chain-smoked, never inhaling when I did, then not smoked at all for ages. Any longevity of my lung function is therefore down to a wonderful mix of eccentricity and stupidity as you might suspect. In fact, stupidity has served me well all my life it seems.

DRAWING: The smokefest. Nige turning pale and wan while I smoke blithely on, indifferent to his suffering. I look handsome and sort of cool in a naff way. Dimps surround us, some of them still alight and perilously near the tent which could have gone up in flames.

Thanks to the likes of John Lennon, macrobiotic diets of fish, rice and whole grains led to a bout of 'right on' health freakism in those days. Nige was a disciple and imbued 'healthy' food with psychedelic qualities. Pink Floyd had singles out then and one of them in particular assumed an absurd importance in his mixed up mind. It wasn't one of the better known hits, *See Emily Play* or *Arnold Layne*, but their forgotten, straight-down-the-pan third single *Apples and Oranges*. These humble, Syd Barrett prescribed fruits became ambrosia in Nige's eyes. He had to eat at least one of each every day to achieve longevity, inner peace and be sure his head was 'where it's at' - wherever that might be.

On the third day at Retchington Hugeley we ran out of fruit and a two-mile trip to the village stores beckoned. Nige, probably from spending too much time with Smartie, had developed a cunning streak. He was still smarting (pun intended but dismal) from his sickening defeat in the smokefest and itching for revenge in the strangest places - often in the tent at night. Towards that end, he bet I couldn't run the two miles to the village, buy apples and oranges from the shop and get back to camp in half

an hour. Even I realised the odds and a bagful of heavy fruit were against

me but he goaded me with the old 'you're chicken' jibe. After three

seconds of careful thought I took on the challenge - in the knowledge that

I could buy apples and oranges from a farm along the way and halve the

distance I'd have to run. It would be a doddle to spike old Nige and

astound the pair of them. My confidence knew no bounds and I even

agreed never to eat a pastie again if I lost and make bacon buttie breakfasts

for Smartie and Nige every morning for the rest of the trip. My reward for

winning was bragging rights and the satisfaction of being intolerably

smug in their company. Yes, it was a crap deal but, remember, I was

dumber than them. That afternoon, in weak sunshine and wearing a T Rex

T-shirt and puce coloured running shorts, I prepared for the Retchington

run. I even brought along my lucky Timex watch which I had to carry in

my pocket as the strap had broken. I tried to act cool but failed as I knew I

was going to win. This puzzled the prickly pair who held a short,

whispered conversation inside the tent. I bent an ear to the flap and heard

every word.

'I don't get it,' began Smartie.

'He thinks he's going to do it,' said Nige.

'What's his game? Simon's keeping something under wraps, methinks.'

They pondered.

'I know,' said Nige.

'What?'

'He's going to cheat.'

'Of course,' said Smartie. 'But how?'

I couldn't be bothered listening in to the rest of their powwow but when they finally emerged the grin on my face was as wide as an open door. I was going to enjoy this and no mistake. But Smartie, living up to his name for once, had been thinking. I was about to set off when he dropped a resounding bombshell bigger than anything since the Blitz and blew my whole plan apart.

'Simon…'

'Yes , mate,' I replied, running confidently on the spot and full of myself.

'When you get to the village make a note of the name above the shop. Me and Nige were there a few days ago when you stayed in camp. If you can't tell us the name you lose - end of.'

'That's ridiculous!' I yelled in protest, well aware of the implications. It was one huge game changer for sure.

DRAWING: Smartie and Nige bowling huge apples and oranges at skittles - all of which feature my fizzog and are being scattered everywhere.

Ashen-faced and deflated, I started off in the direction of Retchington Hugeley feeling like I had lead weights on the end of my legs. Assured victory had turned to embarrassing, inevitable defeat. I had literally been outsmarted and my big chance of getting one up (perhaps an unfortunate turn of phrase) on the two them had faded like the shine on schoolboys' shoes.

I was jogging dispiritedly along the roller coaster road which was a series of formidable ups and knee-pounding downs about a mile from camp when the sun decided to come on strong in a cloudless sky. Sweat and failure seeped from every pore and my mood deteriorated from depressive to manic and panic. The prospect, despite recent events, of a pastieless future watching Smartie and Nige chomping triumphantly on my bacon butts every morning suddenly seemed unbearable. I stopped for a fag, then realised I'd left the packet of Consulate in the tent. It was my lowest point - at the top of a hill. With half a mind (at a guess) not to bother, I set off again on my hopeless quest without the slightest inkling that, actually, it was my lucky day. A local yokel suddenly appeared on the otherwise empty horizon riding a bike and heading in my direction. I flagged him down - even without one.

'You couldn't tell me the name of the grocer's shop in the village,' I enquired.

'You mean Foy's?'

'Do I?'

'I reckon. It's been Foy's these twenty years or more,' he assured me.

'You've made my day.'

'Glad to hear it. I'll be off then.' He pedalled away post-haste shaking his head - obviously in a hurry to leave the weirdo jogger far behind. I diverted to the nearby farm where I secured Nige's psychedelic apples and oranges at a good, ie cheap, price before ambling back to the campsite. There were two minutes and twenty-five seconds left of my half hour when I arrived.

Smartie and Nige took defeat badly. They sussed that I'd cheated but even Smartie never figured out how. Almost fifty years later he regurgitated the subject which is a long time keeping it in there bloating your psyche. Even then, I never let on about the bumpkin and the bike. Getting the hump, he called me a bastard for the one hundred and fiftieth time since I'd known him (yes, I've kept count). That still left him way behind - I've called him the same three times as much. Back at the tent, I was cool, unperturbed, urbane and supremely smug, knowing I'd stitched them both up like a patch on a pair of trousers. Life, at least for the time being, was a gas again.

DRAWING: Me striking a victory pose holding a flag sporting the legend *FOYLED* in large letters.

Smutterington House near our campsite was something of an enigma. Nobody knows how it got its name (although, as the author, I've a pretty good idea) and describing itself as a house must be the euphemism of all time. The place is a palace and probably grander than Lizzie's in London. As for myself, I imagined a portly Lord Smutt in residence with his good lady wife and several football teams of obsequious servants but it turned out that Smutterington House was in fact a National Trust property preserved for the nation. The trust's motto is 'For ever, for everyone'. I imagined my bit as being a miniscule piece of grout in a tiled bathroom wall.

Smutterington's extensive grounds encompassed a large chunk of Yorkshire the size of Batley, Wakefield and Beverley put together. Lakes; parterres; fountains; ha-has; woodlands; fields; rills and streams abounded. Avenues of pleached limes lead to astounding vistas in every direction. (Loving the word, I have never looked up or googled pleached as I don't want to be disappointed). One helluvah place then and open to the public from ten to five on weekdays and Saturday mornings at Lord Trust's discretion.

Smartie suggested we visit and, in a moment of ineffable boredom or tripping out on psychedelic Pomagne, Nige and I agreed to give it the once-over. We'd been through the spectacular Long Gallery, marvelled at endless rooms stuffed with all sorts of treasures and medieval goodies when, finally, we arrived at the Smutts' bedchamber - a splendidly preserved melange of aristocratic bad taste unrivalled on the planet. Nothing matched or seemed much in harmony but, blimey, you just knew everything must have cost a fortune.

We turned to leave when the National Trust guide appeared and immediately focused our attention - on herself. Typically of testosterone-fuelled teenagers, all thoughts of the raven-haired Amber from the Barmaid's Arms were instantly cast aside at the sight of this blonde vision, soon to be the new object of our lovelorn ambition. Her ID tag blazed her name into our consciousness - Anne - which, just there and then, seemed incredibly rare and exotic. Maybe it was that feminine 'e' on the end? To my mind, truncated Anns seem sadly lacking (of an 'e' mainly). She was another 'A' like Amber but, in her case, an A+++++. I suppose she might have had a more colourful name like Arabella, Alethea or Alona but Anne was okay by us even followed, as it was, by the prosaic Smith surname. Oddly enough, we had a classmate in the South Chadd sinkhole of the same name which might have been a remarkable coincidence had they both been called Vashti Titterington.

Author's note: *If you are reading this and your name is in fact Vashti Titterington, my apologies, but I deny your existence utterly.*

As the twittering crowd leaked from the room we looked at each other. One look, Nige's, said 'Who's going to engage this beauty in meaningful conversation'. Another, mine, said 'She's just wonderful!'. A third, Smartie's, said 'Wow! I'd give her one!'. He might have been clever (and the jury's still out on that one) but there was no doubting my friend had the morals of a randy polecat on Viagra. No sheep was safe in his vicinity. Needless to say though, he was the one who successfully chatted her up and, incredibly, she agreed to meet us that evening with two of her friends from the youth club at the large, ornate fountain on the roller coaster road.

'Bags I, Anne!' exclaimed Smartie, as we got ready for our triple date with destiny later on.

'You can't 'bags' a girl, you twonk,' I replied. 'It's down to who she fancies.'

'I chatted her up,' he pointed out.

'You nearly blew it with "Hiya, darlin'. Me and my mates think you're girl lava – really hot!",said Nige. 'Memorable. But for all the wrong reasons.'

'While Anne was talking to you she was looking at us,' I reminded Smartie.

'Probably just feelin' sorry for her friends, knowing they'd be stuck with you two muppets,' he chided.

'Thank you, Kermit.'

'And goodnight!' added Nige, chomping on his third apple of the day and acting all spaced out by the time he reached the core.

DRAWING: Lord Smutt, wearing a monocle and crown, together with Lady Smutt and their extensive brood of little Smutterlings. They have come alive in the huge picture of them above the four poster bed. They are looking down on all of us visitors and spitting feathers at what they regard as an unforgivable intrusion.

We set off down the roller coaster road that evening in good time to meet up with the girls. It would have been cool to be a tad late but none of us were risking that. I'd washed my mod-cut styled hair with Vosene to mitigate dandruff disaster and sprayed gallons of Right Guard under my arms as most guys did then 'on the pull'. Flared blue jeans and a psychedelic shirt with round edges to the collar and images nicked from a Lava Lamp were my cool gear. Smartie was similarly attired but Nige preferred the late 50s Beatnik look - skinny black jeans and turtleneck sweater topped with a comical black beret. His supposedly cool dark glasses had been left behind in the 'Barmaid's' and Amber, as the new owner, was probably looking sensational in them. Traffic's *Hole in My*

Shoe was playing on the small state-of-the-smart transistor radio Smartie had borrowed from Nige to "increase his cool" as he put it - the legendary pranny with a tranny.

We arrived at the fountain with ten minutes to spare. Nige couldn't resist sipping the water gurgling out of a desultory cherub's mouth while we hung around wondering if Anne and her friends would actually turn up.

'PSY-CHE-DEL-IC!' yelled Nige, frightening a flock of sheep in a nearby field and deafening the cherub. Smartie and I were uncomprehending.

'The water,' said Nige, 'it's mind-blowing. Try it, man!' With nothing better to do and no sheep to watch, we did. To our surprise it did taste somehow weird and our imaginations proceeded to run riot. Soon, the three of us were looning about the place, barging into each other, overbalancing and generally behaving like lunatics. Of course, the girls chose that moment to put in an appearance.

'Sorry! Got carried away there,' blurted out Smartie, taking deep breaths as he calmed down. Following suit, Nige and I grinned inanely.

'What was THAT all about?' chorused the girls. They were almost in unison, like they'd been practicing.

'The water from the fountain - it's psychedelic,' explained Nige.

'It does taste…different,' I agreed. With raised eyebrows accompanying their shaking heads, the girls didn't seem too impressed.

'That's probably the extra ingredient,' said Anne, looking stunning in figure-hugging black trousers and a white silk blouse topped with a red neckerchief.

'What extra ingredient?' I wondered aloud.

'Oh, nothing,' she replied, mysteriously, before introducing her two none-too-shabby friends, Pam and Nan. The youth club in the village beckoned where we laughed and chatted over Cokes, coffees and Nan's mam's fruit scones which went down rather better than the music. They were still playing *Rock Around The Clock* and, naff but appropriate, Cliff Richard's *Summer Holiday.*

'You girls should form a group,' advised Smartie, trying to impress whilst feeding the feminine ego. 'Pam, Nan and Anne, the new Supremes. Diana Ross eat your heart out!' Later, he and Anne had a game of table tennis and she wiped the floor with him. Thinking we were on to a winner, we suggested darts and soon wished we hadn't. Battling against the girls, we found we couldn't live with them. They were impressing US.

Suddenly (and totally unexpectedly), Anne took my arm and dragged me outside.

'Fancy a walk in the forest?' she asked. Naturally, I had no objections. Then, reluctantly, I remembered Smartie and Nige.

'Shouldn't we say goodbye?'

'No need. Pam and Nan will look after your friends.'

DRAWING: The three of us looning around at the fountain - the girls giggling nearby. A paling sun above has Syd Barrett's face smiling down on us and, yes, The Madcap is indeed laughing.

Blokeism - it's a strange phenomenon. The banter and camaraderie, all for one and one for all, friends forever and the like. Then; the female of the species comes along and it's suddenly every man for himself and peacock feathers out to beguile the new arrival. I knew Smartie would be seething and Nige none too pleased as Anne and I disappeared along the bridle path into the forest but, sadly, I didn't give a monkey's (being Simon of that ilk). Smartie being one (and a superior one at that) had always assumed that the geek would inherit the Earth, or whatever he fancied standing upon it. Well; not this time, matey. Shockingly and against all expectations beauty had chosen the least likely lad - and was walking away with her prize, such as it was.

Shafts of weak sunlight breaking through the interstices of the trees above illuminated our way. We wandered along hand in hand, sharing the moment wordlessly. A carpet of pine needles underfoot added to the spring in my step before a stile interrupted our progress. On the other side was a low wall and we rested there awhile, her head on my shoulder and my hand moving gently through Anne's long, silken hair - happy together like The Turtles' song.

'Do you know anything about horses?' Anne brought me down to Earth with a bump with that one.

'Of course,' I lied, remembering they had four legs and liked sugar lumps. I kissed her: one for the Hell of it, two as it was deeply pleasurable and three to stifle any further equine enquiries I wouldn't be able to answer. Moving on, we emerged from the trees into a quiet country lane with a field opposite dotted with small fences and some stables at the far end.

Anne crossed over and opened the gate.

'Come on. I'll show you Buster.'

'This lot's yours then?'

'Rented, I'm afraid.'

At the stables, Buster seemed pleased to see her though he eyed me suspiciously I thought. He was a grey, medium-sized beastie and, at least according to Anne, "as gentle as a lamb".

'You're welcome to take him round the course,' she told me, indicating the fences we'd passed along the way. By then, I'd already claimed to have ridden before and had painted myself into a very uncomfortable corner. Like the dumb ass I was, I felt I had no option but to give it a go. Climbing aboard with difficulty (it would have been easier on my own), I took the reins with some trepidation. I was wearing Anne's riding hat which was a size too small and made me look stupid - as if I needed any help. Approaching the first fence, about a foot high, the horse suddenly baulked at the prospect and I fell off spectacularly, rolling in a crumpled heap on the ground. Buster looked down on me mockingly, neigh disdainfully, and sauntered haughtily back to his stable. Anne was distraught and shaking her head.

'You can't ride, can you Simon…Are you hurt?'

'Arm and ribs a little; pride a lot,' I answered, conjuring up a smile from the depths of my humiliation.

'Come on!' She helped me to my feet and led me to the gate. After securing the aptly-named Buster in his stable she returned and took me home for repairs which, luckily, were minor. They were administered expertly by her mum who was clearly used to that sort of thing. I didn't know then, of course, but my friends hadn't fared much better elsewhere that evening.

Back at the youth club and tired of losing at everything Smartie and Nige persuaded Pam and Nan to return to the fountain and sample the psychedelic water for themselves.

'Just one thing boys,' said Pam, when they arrived.

'It really is psychedelic,' Nige assured them.

'I don't doubt it,' agreed Nan. 'But you do know, don't you?'

'What?' said Smartie.

'People…revellers, holidaymakers and the like, they've been known to, well…'

'Relieve themselves in the fountain,' interrupted Pam. Nige, who had just swallowed another handful of water, retched horribly while Smartie was mightily relieved (oh, gawd) not to have followed Nige's example.

'Hey, girls, come on. That's in poor taste,' he quipped, his savoir faire fully restored. Nige's face had turned the ghastly yellow of urine as the girls wept with laughter but Smartie was merciless.

'Serves him right - taking the piss!'

'I know what will cheer him up,' announced Pam. The two girls marched Smartie and a down-in-the-mouth Nige to the river flowing gently through the grounds of Smutterington House. A large and roomy rowing boat was tied to a post by a painter (probably a watercolourist - a descendant of Cezanne). They got the boat out and, with Nan and Nige at the oars and Smartie and Pam snuggled together on the rear seat, headed downstream. This required little effort by anyone and Nan and Nige soon abandoned the oars in favour of introducing their tonsils to each other. The kisses may have been French but it was an earthy English embrace all right. Nan had forgotten or didn't care any longer what Nige had been drinking. Nige, enjoying the moment, would undoubtedly have said 'psychedelic' - if he could have said anything at all.

While everyone was enjoying themselves under a starry summer sky the boat drifted lazily onwards before seeming to pick up speed. It soon became obvious why. The moonlight picked out a weir a short distance ahead. Smartie leapt forward, pushing Nan and Nige unceremoniously out of the way, and took up the oars. Sadly, it was way too late.

'Jump! Head for the banking,' he yelled. As they threw themselves overboard the boat listed doing everyone a favour and tipping them out just in time. Within seconds, it had disappeared over the weir at a rate of knots never to be seen again - at least by any of the boating party.

DRAWING: The two couples snogging in the boat as it picks up speed near the weir. A sign sticking out of the water reads 'ROW NOW…..THE OTHER WAY YOU IDIOT!'. Another sign, closer to the edge of the weir, reads 'TOO LATE!'.

THE END

www.ingramcontent.com/pod-product-compliance
Lightning Source LLC
Chambersburg PA
CBHW081202280526

45791CB00006B/2158